Managing the Flexible Workforce

Richard Pettinger

- Fast track route to the effective management of flexible workers and working arrangements

- Covers the key areas of managing the flexible workforce from attitude formation, leadership, direction and motivation to group management and flexible workforce development

- Examples and lessons from some of the world's most successful businesses including Sandals Inc, British Airways, Cobra Beer, and Semco, and ideas from the smartest thinkers including Peter Drucker, Peter Senge, Linda Gratton and Robert Heller

- Includes a glossary of key concepts and a comprehensive resources guide

PEOPLE

09.08

>>EXPRESS EXEC.COM<<
essential management thinking at your fingertips

The right of Richard Pettinger to be identified as the author of this work has been asserted in accordance with the Copyright, Designs and Patents Act 1988

First published 2002 by
Capstone Publishing (a Wiley company)
8 Newtec Place
Magdalen Road
Oxford OX4 1RE
United Kingdom
http://www.capstoneideas.com

CIP catalogue records for this book are available from the British Library and the US Library of Congress

ISBN 1-84112-248-3

This book is printed on acid-free paper

Substantial discounts on bulk quantities of Capstone books are available to corporations, professional associations and other organizations. Please contact Capstone for more details on +44 (0)1865 798 623 or (fax) +44 (0)1865 240 941 or (e-mail) info@wiley-capstone.co.uk

Contents

Introduction to

ExpressExec

ExpressExec is 3 million words of the latest management thinking compiled into 10 modules. Each module contains 10 individual titles forming a comprehensive resource of current business practice written by leading practitioners in their field. From brand management to balanced scorecard, ExpressExec enables you to grasp the key concepts behind each subject and implement the theory immediately. Each of the 100 titles is available in print and electronic formats.

Through the ExpressExec.com Website you will discover that you can access the complete resource in a number of ways:

» printed books or e-books;
» e-content – PDF or XML (for licensed syndication) adding value to an intranet or Internet site;
» a corporate e-learning/knowledge management solution providing a cost-effective platform for developing skills and sharing knowledge within an organization;
» bespoke delivery – tailored solutions to solve your need.

Why not visit www.expressexec.com and register for free key management briefings, a monthly newsletter and interactive skills checklists. Share your ideas about ExpressExec and your thoughts about business today.

Please contact elound@wiley-capstone.co.uk for more information.

Introduction to Flexible Working

» The drive is towards flexibility, dynamism and responsiveness – qualities that lead to increased levels of customer service.
» Flexible working is not new. It has been adopted in health, energy, transport and emergency services; multinational companies locating in different parts of the world; small and medium-sized enterprises; and consultancies and agencies.
» The drive for flexibility, dynamism and responsiveness is based on a combination of that which exists already, and the potential for future development and improvement.

Everywhere in the world there is a revolution going on, a transformation of business, and of the services needed and wanted by people. There is a realization that, however organizational activities were arranged and conducted in the past, new and better methods are essential for the future. This means a better understanding of the nature of work; the needs of all organizations to get the most from their resources - including their people; and to devise work methods and working patterns which fit into all of this.

THE DRIVE FOR FLEXIBLE WORKING

The drive is towards flexibility, dynamism and responsiveness - qualities that lead to increased levels of customer service. This is brought about by changing levels of customer expectations, much of which has happened as the result of improvements in product quality and levels of services deriving from technological advance and successful organization in some sectors. Public service resource pressures are a real problem, and this is certain to continue for the foreseeable future.

Flexible attitudes and approaches to work are designed to address some of these issues. At their heart lies the needs of organizations to maintain long-term existence, success, profitability and effectiveness in a rapidly changing and turbulent world. The best way to do this is to:

» ensure that the people concerned have the necessary skills, qualities, attitudes and approaches to work;
» attend to the demands of specific customers and clients; and
» create work methods and patterns that are suitable to product and service delivery, and which meet the demands of customers and clients.

THE ROOTS OF FLEXIBLE WORKING

Flexible working, in itself, is not new.

» Health, energy, transport and emergency services have always had to be available 24 hours a day, seven days a week, all year round to meet the needs of those using them. Unconventional and irregular patterns of work have therefore existed in these sectors for a very long time.

» Multinational companies locating in different parts of the world have always had to adjust their methods of work to take account of local customs and pressures.

» Small and medium-sized enterprises have long had to adopt flexibility as an attitude. Whether in response to one-off requests or producing specialist items, their existence has always depended on producing client and customer satisfaction in these circumstances.

» Consultancies and agencies have to work on the premise that each new problem, request or issue that comes to them will be unique, different, specialized and have its own particular set of circumstances. Again, therefore, it has always been necessary to adapt particular expertise to changing sets of circumstances so that effective and profitable responses are always given.

CONCLUSIONS

The drive for flexibility, dynamism and responsiveness is based on a combination of that which exists already, and the potential for future development and improvement. Part of this relates to ever-more detailed attention to costs and investment, and the need to gain the best value and returns on each. It is also necessary to engage corporate and managerial attitudes, the chief of which is an understanding and acknowledgement of the fact that there are specific types of investment, and specific skills and expertise, that are needed in flexible working situations.

What is Flexible Working?

» "Flexible working" is the term used to describe the ability to employ people when and where required in the interests of everybody. The broadening of flexible working approaches was boosted in the 1980s by high levels of structural unemployment in many parts of the Western world.

» Because of the rapid pace of innovation and advance, technology and equipment has a much more uncertain useful lifespan than in the past. It is therefore essential to have staff expertise available for as long as possible while it is being used.

» Staff, expertise and resources have to be engaged when and where customers and clients demand, otherwise they will simply go elsewhere.

» Specific demands from the supply side have to be maximized and optimized.

» It is essential for managers to realize that flexible working is a form of organizational investment.

"Flexible working" is the term used to describe the ability to employ people when and where required in the interests of everybody. It involves the creation of work patterns and arrangements based on the need to maximize and optimize organizational output, customer and client satisfaction, and staff expertise and effectiveness. Specific issues that must be addressed are the maximization and optimization of:

» returns on investment in technology, premises and equipment;
» customer and client convenience and requirements; and
» any specific demands from the supply side.

This means that attention is required to the following:

» patterns of work and contractual arrangements; and other formats under which staff are employed;
» organization structure and culture; and
» management priorities.

Flexible working is distinguished from "standard" or "normal hours" working which, in European and North American cultures, is normally taken to mean five days per week, from 9.00 am to 5.00 pm, or the equivalent (see Summary box 2.1).

SUMMARY BOX 2.1: STANDARD HOURS IN PRACTICE

In practice, standard hours and normal patterns of work vary enormously.

» In the UK, the US, Australia, New Zealand and South Africa, they are normally taken to be Monday to Friday, 9.00 am to 5.00 pm. This is in spite of the fact that, in many parts of each of these countries, as many as 40% of the working population do not work these hours.
» In France, most commercial services close on Mondays (for the morning at least) but work Saturday mornings; the only exceptions to this are in the big cities.

» In Italy, Spain and Greece, patterns of work are varied during the summer months so that work is carried out between 7.00 and 11.30 am and between 6.00 and 9.00 pm because of the extremes of hot weather.

» In Asia and the former Communist bloc, the standard hours of work include Saturdays and Sunday mornings (this is also found in local services in countries of the European Union).

In practice, in many parts of the urban US, EU and former Communist bloc, the difference between culture and perception, and practice, is becoming very wide. Staff in many sectors are in fact required to work, or be prepared to work, flexible and often unsocial hours. This is either because of commercial drives – the need to finish projects, attend to increased customer demands, or in the delivery of privatized or commercialized public services; or else it is because customer and client expectations have developed from the point at which they are prepared to continue to do business with those who still operate only standard hours.

RETURN ON INVESTMENT

Because of the rapid pace of innovation and advance, technology and equipment has a much more uncertain useful lifespan than in the past. It is therefore essential to have staff expertise available for as long as possible while it is being used. This involves designing work patterns to ensure that it is used to its full capacity.

A wide range of industrial, commercial and public service occupations now rely on those who have the required capability and willingness to work nights, weekends and split shifts (alternative days/nights) as well as:

» twilight hours, between 5.00 and 12.00 pm in the evening;
» irregular hours which usually have a core period when staff are required to attend, plus additional hours by arrangement/agreement; and
» job-and-finish, of especial importance in IT and some engineering project work when the client requires express or urgent delivery.

Handy: the core and peripheral workforce

In *The Age of Unreason* (Penguin, 1990), C.B. Handy identified "the shamrock organization" as shown in the first part of Fig. 2.1. Handy used this to explain the need for a core – requiring permanence, stability and order. The core is responsible for organizing the rest of the work around the different areas according to commercial demands. Handy draws special attention to the use of subcontractors and consultants as a strategic process. These are experts required from time to time to whom high fees (economic rent) are paid in return for instant, top-quality response and service.

(a) *The Shamrock Model*

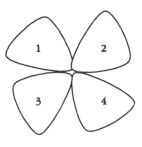

1   The core

2   Specialists

3   Seasonal staff

4   Staff on retainers for pressures and emergencies

(b) *The Propeller Model*

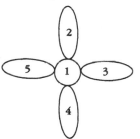

1   The core
2   Specialists
3   Subcontractors
4   Research and development
5   Seasonal staff

Fig. 2.1   Core and periphery. (Source: Handy, C.B., 1990, *The Age of Unreason*, Penguin.)

This may be contrasted with the Japanese/Korean *keiretsu* and *chaebol* models, in which organizations seek to employ everyone required, and to integrate them into large conglomerates. They then base this on fully flexible working practices (see below) and use the full-time availability of expertise to develop new business opportunities.

Some authorities add a fifth element to Handy's model, so that "the core" remains at the center. This is depicted in the second part of Fig. 2.1 (the propeller model).

MAXIMIZING AND OPTIMIZING CUSTOMER AND CLIENT SERVICE

Technological advances, increasing competitiveness and the globalization of many sectors have led to greatly enhanced choices for all products and services on the part of customers and clients. Increased expectations for product and service quality, durability and convenience have led people to seek out any organization from anywhere that is capable and willing to provide this.

The consequence is that staff, expertise and resources have to be engaged when and where customers and clients demand, otherwise they will simply go elsewhere. It follows from this that the future of many organizations is dependent on their capability to find high-quality staff willing to work when required (see Summary box 2.2)

SUMMARY BOX 2.2: PRIORITIES

Graham Manuel graduated from University College London with a first-class degree. He was engaged as a trainee consultant by McKinsey, the top-brand global management consultants.

The company paid him extremely well and agreed with him an extensive training and development plan, and initial client portfolio.

Graham was also a brilliant hockey player. He continued to play for the University of London, one of the UK's top clubs. One Saturday at half-time during a game, his secretary arrived with an air ticket to New York. A client wished to see him first thing the following day (Sunday). He accordingly had to leave the game and go directly to Heathrow in order to catch the last plane to new York that day.

MAXIMIZING AND OPTIMIZING SPECIFIC DEMANDS FROM THE SUPPLY SIDE

This requires the capability to design work patterns around the need for particular supplies (both physical and virtual), and when these can best be delivered to everyone's advantage.

It also depends on the strategic approach taken. This is a key issue where just-in-time (JiT) is involved – the practice of having small regular deliveries that can then go straight into production or usage, thus obviating the need for extensive and expensive stockpiling and storage. In certain industries there is the additional need to keep stocks of foodstuffs and other perishable goods fresh (see Summary box 2.3).

Finally, organizations need the ability to download particular data and information as soon as it becomes available, and to access databases anywhere in the world where required when they are open.

SUMMARY BOX 2.3: JIT AND TRANSPORT PROBLEMS

The key drive in establishing supply side flexibility in many urbanized parts of the US, EU and Far East is traffic congestion. The road network is so overcrowded and overloaded that this has caused both manufacturing and retail organizations to look at the use of the period 10.00 pm to 6.00 am to make their major deliveries. Supplementaries only are made during the rest of the day. It is impossible to rely on the transport network to remain uncongested for long enough to ensure reliability on the supply side outside these hours.

CORPORATE RESPONSIBILITY

The broadening of flexible working approaches was boosted in the 1980s by high levels of structural unemployment in many parts of the Western world. Many organizations were therefore able to demand their own prescribed patterns of work, in return for pay rates that they were able to impose. This meant:

» the principle of flexible working became very much more widely known, perceived, understood and accepted;
» many jobs were taken only under duress because people could not find anything else; and
» staff tended to be treated on a casual and unvalued basis.

In many occupations (e.g. garment manufacture, telesales) staff effectively became a commodity, working long and unsocial hours in return for low wages. In the short term, people would remain in these jobs only until alternatives presented themselves. In the long term, companies that did not greatly increase the value placed on capability and willingness found themselves losing reputation and identity, and therefore competitive edge, at exactly the same time that competition was globalizing (see Summary box 2.4).

SUMMARY BOX 2.4: RECEIVED AND HOMESPUN WISDOM

The perception that staff could be treated as a commodity was reinforced by the then received management "wisdom" that: "If you do not want this job, there are 20 million others who do."

Working in organizations that adopt this corporate attitude reduces individual and collective self-respect and self-worth. There is no possibility of a long-term mutually productive or profitable relationship (even if, in the short term, it clearly works to an extent). High-quality high-value work for low wages is sustainable only in the short term (see also Chapter 5). If wages are not raised, the quality and value of the work itself declines, and this is compounded by the fact that there is no quality of working life or relationship on which to rebuild.

CONCLUSIONS

It is essential for managers to realize that flexible working is a form of organizational investment the purpose of which is to get the best out of existing and finite resources over long periods of time.

Flexible working is therefore not cheap. Some cost savings may be possible in some circumstances. However, it must be remembered, at all times, that the design and development of these approaches and attitudes to working are to be engaged in exactly the same ways as rigid corporate hierarchies were in previous times – the creation of an organization that is capable of meeting production and service requirements, and generating long-term and enduring customer satisfaction.

KEY LEARNING POINTS

- Flexible working should be viewed as part of the corporate approach towards maximizing and optimizing customer/client convenience and satisfaction, and thus maximizing return on investment.
- It requires specific attention to customer and client service.
- It requires specific attention to the supply side.
- There is corporate responsibility towards the welfare of the workforce.

The Evolution of Flexible Working

The evolution of flexible working is studied here under the headings:

» The Industrial Revolution
» Scientific management
» Human relations
» Japanese manufacturing
» Regulation and deregulation
» Overseas sourcing.

As with so much organizational and managerial practice, flexible working has emerged piecemeal rather than as a distinctive and structured, or planned, development. From both the highest and also the lowest of motivations, organizations, their owners and managers have sought to improve capability and value in delivering goods and services to their customers. Key milestones and stages in the development of organizational and managerial approaches to work patterns and arrangements are highlighted in this chapter.

THE INDUSTRIAL REVOLUTION

The population explosions and rapid urbanization that took place from the mid eighteenth century onwards meant that there was an over-supply of labor to those who owned businesses. People used to queue for work every day; and there was therefore a fully flexible, and willing – and entirely captive – workforce.

Marx and Engels (1848) defined this as "wage slavery" – the requirement to sell labor in return for pay without any security or guarantee of continuity of work.

Many industries went a stage further and the human input was provided by slaves who were farmed, bought and sold on the commodities market alongside the crops and products that they themselves subsequently produced.

Neither the practices nor the organizations, nor the general state of civilization, could sustain this. The companies created during the Industrial Revolution that have survived to the present day have done so *without exception* because they were prepared to pay a broader social, as well as economic, attention to the staff and activities (see Summary box 3.1).

SUMMARY BOX 3.1: THE ORIGINS OF WELFARISM

The first industry to make a priority the welfare of its staff was the UK chocolate sector. The Cadbury family who pioneered and built up the chocolate and cocoa industries in the nineteenth century came from a strong religious tradition (they were Quakers).

Determined to be both profitable and ethical, they sought to ensure certain standards of living and quality of life for those who worked for them. They built factories and housing for their staff at a model industrial village at Bourneville on the edge of the city of Birmingham in the UK.

The village included basic housing and sanitation, green spaces, schools for the children and company shops that sold food of a good quality. The purpose was to ensure that the staff were kept fit, healthy and motivated to work in the chocolate factories so that they could produce good quality products.

Other Quaker foundations operated along similar lines, for example the Fry and Terry companies (both also chocolate producers).

SCIENTIFIC MANAGEMENT

The concept of scientific management was pioneered by F.W. Taylor (1856-1917). Scientific management meant taking a precise approach to the problems of work and work organization.

Taylor's hypothesis was based on the premise that proper organization of the workforce and work methods would improve efficiency. The approach was based on a fundamentally cooperative attitude between managers and workers. Work organization should be such that it removed all responsibility from the workers, leaving them only with their particular task. By specializing and training in this task, the individual worker would become perfect in job performance. Work could thus be reorganized into production lines and items produced efficiently and to a constant standard as the result. Precise performance standards would be predetermined by job observation and analysis and a best method arrived at; and this would become the normal way of working.

Everyone would benefit:

» the organization because it cut out all wasteful and inefficient use of resources;

» managers because they had a known standard of work to set and observe; and
» workers because they would always do the job the same way.

Everyone would benefit financially also from the increase in output, sales and profits, and the reflection of this in high wage and salary levels.

At the Bethlehem Steel Works Inc. in the US, Taylor optimized productive labor at the ore and coal stockpiles by providing various sizes of shovels from which the men could choose to ensure that they used whichever was best suited to them. Taylor reduced handling costs per ton by a half over a three-year period; he also reduced the size of the workforce required to do this from 400 to 140.

Taylor's premise was that this degree of specialization would be tolerated by staff in return for enduringly high levels of wages. Breaking every job down into its component parts, and allocating an individual to each part, meant that the organization's production methods became effectively fully flexible. However, despite the enduringly high levels of wages paid, they took no account of the human side of enterprise – the need for variety, enhancement and real and perceived achievement.

HUMAN RELATIONS

The most famous and pioneering work carried out in the field of human relations was the Hawthorne studies at the Western Electric Company in Chicago. These studies were carried out over the period 1924–36. Originally designed to draw conclusions between the working environment and work output, they finished as major studies of work groups, social factors, employee attitudes and values, and the effect of these at places of work.

The Hawthorne Works employed over 30,000 people at the time, making telephone equipment. Elton Mayo, Professor of Industrial Research at Harvard University, was called in to advise the company because there was both poor productivity and a high level of employee dissatisfaction.

One of the approaches was based on the hypothesis that productivity would improve if working conditions were improved. The first stage was the improvement of the lighting for a group of female workers; to give a measure of validity to the results, a control group was established whose lighting was to remain consistent. However, the output of both groups improved, and continued to improve, whether the level of lighting was increased or decreased.

The second element extended the experiments to include rest pauses, variations in starting and finishing times, and in the timing and length of the lunch break. At each stage, the output of both groups rose until the point at which the women in the experimental group complained that they had too many breaks and that their work rhythm was being disrupted.

Other approaches included a major attitude survey of over 20,000 of the company's employees, and in-depth observation of both the informal, and formal, working groups. In 1936, Mayo and his team from Harvard drew all the threads together; and this resulted in the following major conclusions.

» Individuals need to be given importance in their own right and must also be seen as group or team members, as well as organizational employees.
» The need to belong at the workplace is of fundamental importance, as critical in its own way as both pay and rewards, and also working conditions.
» There is both a formal, and informal, organization with formal and informal groups and structures; the informal exerts a strong influence over the formal.
» People respond positively to active involvement in work.
» People respond to having a direct interest taken in their welfare and conditions, as well as their output.

The development of the human relations approach took place over the period between, and after, the two world wars, and across the great depression (1928–31). Part of the more general organization and management thrust at the time was to try to create order and certainty in order to avoid the chaos and deprivation. Accordingly, orderly organization structures, ranking orders and hierarchies were created, providing jobs into which people could enter and be appointed or promoted. These forms of organization would provide stability, certainty and security for all those who worked in them; and this would be ensured by the certainty of stable and growing domestic markets.

The key problem was the concentration on organizational form rather than "pure" human relations or activities. There was a consequent proliferation of non-productive and administrative jobs. The cost of making permanent the rank order and hierarchy was very high, whether this had to be paid for out of sales, goods and services, or from the public purse for education, health, infrastructure and social services.

JAPANESE MANUFACTURING

Over the period since 1960, Japanese industry has transformed its outputs and reputation from low quality and low customer confidence, to high quality and high customer confidence. Japanese companies are now the major supplier of electrical goods to the US, Australia, New Zealand and Western Europe, as well as being major players in the car, computer and banking sectors.

The components of success of the Japanese companies over this period are as follows.

» *Conformity*. This is the requirement to adopt the distinctive standards, attitudes and values of the organization. In order for this to be successful, it requires vision and direction from the top of companies so that it is both profitable and worthy of respect from staff and customers.
» *Adaptation and adaptability*. Very few products made by Japanese companies were invented by them. Japanese technologists, researchers and business developers have seen the potential of existing products and services, and adapted them and commercialized them, often where European and North American companies could see no future or potential.
» *Investment emphasis*. This is on the long-term, rather than immediate, returns. This has allowed companies in all parts of industry and commerce to develop flexibility and confidence, to pioneer, to develop and innovate products and services in the expectation of long-term success and profitability without having short-term financial problems or targets to meet.

» *Investment in staff training*. This is at all levels of the organization. The returns are measurable in relation to employee commitment, positive attitudes, identity rather than alienation, and minute levels of absenteeism, as well as multi-skilling, agreement to full flexibility of working, and capability and willingness in all aspects of product and service delivery.

» *Concentration on, and commitment to, the development of managers and supervisors*. This is especially in the areas of staff management and problem-solving. Most Japanese organizations have no capability to institutionalize problems, disputes or grievances – they require these to be resolved without engaging in forms of conflict and labor relations problems that were so much a feature of the equivalent sectors in the West.

» *Single workplace status*. While there is a strong social hierarchy in Japan, it is reflected at the workplace only to the extent that the senior is worthy of respect. The workplace otherwise requires that this be translated into business needs only, and in this situation everyone is important in their role, whatever that may be. It is usual for everyone to wear the same uniform and to go through the same basic induction, orientation and core training program, to use the same facilities, and to be on the same basic terms and conditions of employment.

» *A strong identity*. All staff are required to identify strongly with the company. In managerial and professional occupations, this may involve working very long hours, taking an active part in corporate hospitality and business-related activities in the evening. Activities designated "voluntary" are not voluntary to such staff in Japanese companies. These organizations insist on high levels of active loyalty and commitment in return for the commitment to lifetime employment.

REGULATION AND DEREGULATION

The approaches to labor markets in the EU and US have been very different. The EU has sought to legislate for all areas, occupations, locations and patterns of work to ensure fundamental standards of pay, conditions and security. In contrast, the US has deregulated its labor markets to make work available to as wide a range of people as possible subject only to the willingness to agree a rate of pay.

In terms of long-term survival, effectiveness, success and profitability, however, the end result has been the same. Companies that survive and prosper in both regulated and deregulated labor markets do so because of their own active responsibility and quality of management, not because of regulation or lack of it. The need to provide adequate levels of pay, reward and security transcend the laws of particular countries. A key to the success of Japanese manufacturing companies is the extent to which their quality of working life, intrinsic interest and workplace security have fitted in and been acceptable everywhere.

OVERSEAS SOURCING

Other organizations have taken the view that flexibility refers to the management of the supply side as the key to securing long-term prosperity. The following approaches are apparent.

» *Moral pricing.* Third world sources are used and the organization undertakes to pay Western prices for their usage. For example, Body Shop uses a wide diversity of sources for the crops that it needs to produce its organic cosmetics, toiletries and gift ranges, and agrees to pay Western prices for these in all cases.

» *Legal pricing.* Third world sources are used and the organization undertakes to pay the local legal rates for their usage. For example, Nike has established a code of conduct requiring all its suppliers to pay at least the local minimum wage in their factories, not to employ underage labor, and to give adequate breaks, working conditions and education for those still of school age.

» *Transfer pricing.* The organization uses third world sources and agrees to pay in Western, rather than local, currency.

» *Expedient pricing and producer relationships.* The organization buys from the supplier without reference to the conditions under which the goods or crops were produced.

» *Extreme dominance-dependency.* The organization comes to dominate the producer or supplier and then drives down the price that it pays (see Summary box 3.2).

SUMMARY BOX 3.2: OVERSEAS SOURCING

All the big Western sports and leisurewear companies use third world suppliers to some extent and, from time to time, there have been scandals concerning this. Adidas and Reebok both admitted to taking supplies from factories staffed by child labor in Pakistan and Bangladesh. Nike drew up its code of conduct after complaints about working practices in factories used by the company in Cambodia and Vietnam. Even Body Shop, which takes a high-profile ethical stance, has caused indigenous economic problems where it has found itself unable, or unwilling, to purchase crops previously acquired following changes in production lines and consumer tastes.

CONCLUSIONS

Rather than attending to flexible working in terms of work patterns, it is more suitable to see this development as a response to competitive and commercial pressures on the one hand, and organizational shortcomings on the other. The work patterns have emerged as the result of these elements and of the economic conditions in which they occurred. In the pursuit of effective long-term flexible working, it is essential that organizations understand that the attitudes and practices adopted have human relations, as well as operational and competitive, needs. It is also essential to understand that if one of these elements is ineffective then the whole is diluted.

KEY LEARNING POINTS

- » Some firms have found it expedient to treat staff as a commodity.
- » The development of human relations and the paternalism of Cadbury and others sowed the seeds of a more enlightened view.
- » Flexibility can be seen as a state of mind.
- » Flexibility can also be linked to a return on investment.
- » There are opportunities in all situations and labor markets.
- » Attention is required to staff and management development.
- » There is a necessity for corporate responsibility.

The E-Dimension of
Flexible Working

» The e-dimension of flexible working is discussed here under the headings:
  » E-mail
  » Internet access
  » Portability
  » Other factors.
» Best-practice case: Management Studies Centre of University College London.

The availability of the Internet as a medium in which to conduct business and as an additional means of developing organizational and staff capability and processes has brought a range of potential opportunities and consequences for flexible working.

The fundamental effectiveness of Web usage in flexible working lies in recognizing that the technology is a tool and support function for the work and not the driving force. It is completely legitimate to ask the questions:

» "What opportunities does the Web bring?" and
» "How may these be exploited and maximized?"

but organizations must be prepared to accept the full range of possible answers. In many cases, these include acknowledging that there are no opportunities for virtual work in the particular situation.

Some more or less universal opportunities are available for the effective use and development of flexible working, as well as specific applications.

E-MAIL

Used properly, high-quality and precisely directed e-mail communications enable everyone to receive and analyze the same information, whatever their location, pattern or hours of work. This also applies to general delivery of information including "all-staffers."

Problems arise when it becomes known, believed or perceived that general information is being propagated very much in the interest of the core workforce or those on full-time and regularized patterns of work. Those away from the organization for long periods of time, or during regular hours, come to wonder what is going on and whether there are things in which they should be taking a greater interest.

In these cases, feelings of alienation and isolation begin to develop. These are compounded if adequate access to managerial and institutional support is not available. This leads to the beginnings of:

» anxieties about job and work security;
» feelings that what is being achieved by the flexible workforce is being frittered away by those at corporate headquarters;

» cluster groups of flexible workers and other staff that turn into corporate moaning and grievance sessions; and
» proliferation of management time and expense reassuring flexible and non-standard staff that they are reading the wrong things into the situation.

This, again, reinforces the need for distinctive qualities in organizational, managerial and supervisory support for those on flexible work patterns. E-mail and Web-based outputs must be capable of quick and positive assimilation by all concerned. Where it comes to be known, believed or perceived that mixed messages are being given out, managers and supervisors have clear duties (and need the capability to be able) to explain what is being said, why and by whom, and what this means to those on non-standard working arrangements.

INTERNET ACCESS

Preaching perfection, this should be made available to everyone on the same basis, regardless of rank, status, hours or patterns of work. In practice, this is rarely possible in absolute terms. Websites and intranets must therefore be capable of universal workforce access as and when required, including from non-organizational equipment such as that available at business centers and Internet cafés. Any charges incurred at the point of access should be reimbursed.

This also applies to factory staff and those engaged in supply, retail and distribution. Where PCs or laptops are not provided, then universality is achieved through the provision of open access equipment in common areas and restrooms, and partly also through privately owned equipment. Again, in the latter case, charges incurred should be reimbursed (see Summary box 4.1).

SUMMARY BOX 4.1: MARKS & SPENCER IN FRANCE

Marks & Spencer, the UK-based international department store chain, became embroiled in declining business performance and reputation among customers, suppliers, the media and analysts over the period 1998–2001.

As part of a restructuring exercise, it decided to close its 12 stores in France in March 2001. The company posted details on its own staff Website. French and international news media quickly got hold of the story and this was duly broadcast on the same evening.

For staff arriving home from their work at the stores, this was the first that they had heard of it. It quickly became apparent that the company had not followed up or supported the Website briefing with information or instructions to department store managers or supervisors, nor had any other information been published.

Accordingly, the staff invoked French labor laws and gained a court ruling that the stores must be reopened while full consultation took place.

Because of the adverse media reaction, the company's reputation – already suffering because of declining sales – was further damaged. Fewer people than ever chose to take their custom to the company.

Mismanagement of the e-dimension regarding the communications aspect of the organization therefore had a direct effect on overall performance, customer values and broader company reputation, as well as being extremely damaging to staff morale.

PORTABILITY

Because so much technology is portable, in many cases work can be conducted at any time from any location. It can also be commanded at short notice when required. Those who do not have PC or laptop equipment can easily get access through computer centers and Internet cafés, where whatever is required can be hired by the hour or on a job-and-finish basis.

This gives great opportunities for flexibility and responsiveness, and is of especial value to those in professional services (e.g. architecture, design, planning, business and management consultancy) when clients may suddenly want information or specifications at times to suit them.

It is also useful in the contracting out of administration, finance and other support functions, when again, management information can be called up for comment and analysis when required.

Portability also brings derived advantages to flexible workers in terms of balancing their job with other life demands. Those with young children can set aside hours to suit them, and put in a full and effective contribution when their time and energy is not otherwise taken up – provided that the organization, and its customer and client demands, permit.

Again, however, there is a corporate moral and ethical responsibility attached. Some of these elements are indeed effective in many cases. However, others working in flexible patterns based on technological portability and universality of access have complained of increased work pressures and demands as the result (see Summary box 4.2).

SUMMARY BOX 4.2: TECHNOLOGY, FLEXIBILITY AND WORKING LIFE IN THE CITY OF LONDON

The report sponsored by the Chartered Institute of Management Accountants, and carried out by City Research Group Ltd in September 2000, questioned 400 senior executives from international companies in the City of London and asked them to predict areas of future success and failure, working conditions, education, the impact of technology and the changing shape of the working environment. Some of the findings were as follows.

» Only 5% of responses mentioned e-business or commerce as a truly important factor affecting future success. Technology was found to have an impact on working conditions, and 60% claimed that technological advance had led to increases in workload.

» Education was considered a crucial factor in shaping the future business world. Many believed that education had to keep up with changing business needs, with the emphasis on leadership and communication skills, rather than IT and technological proficiency.

» The major issue was found to be the ability to recruit and retain high-quality and expert staff. However, it was apparent that few organizations had any conception of how to do this – fewer than 1% of those responding viewed human resource management or labor relations policies as making a key or critical contribution to this.

» The survey also found that senior executives in France and Germany had the shortest working weeks and best work/life balance. Compared with senior UK executives working an average of 55 hours per week, French and German business leaders average only 47. However, only one-third of UK companies said they did anything to fight work-induced stress or other problems associated with long hours of working.

Sources: City Research Group Ltd (2000) "Success beyond 2000," CIMA; Ledger, W. (2000) "How technology has made our lives busier," *London Evening Standard*.

OTHER FACTORS

The other factors that have to be considered when assessing the effects of the e-dimension on flexible working include the following.

Website design

In terms of the contribution of effective flexible working, the essential elements are the following.

» The site should be easy to access and navigate, with attention to security and password arrangements, effectiveness of sign-posting, availability and access to information in the forms required, whatever the location or hours of work. This requires supporting those affected with extensive and continuing training and development, as well as receptiveness to suggestions and contributions from those who use the site. Those on non-standard hours or patterns of attendance might also reasonably expect some say in what information was made available, when and in what format.

» Attention must be paid to working conditions, especially for those attending irregularly or out of normal hours. Unsupported twilight, night and weekend working at which operators sit at their workstations without recourse to facilities such as coffee and cafeteria quickly come to feel undervalued, both in absolute terms and in ways relative to others on perceived standard hours and patterns of work.
» Information should be current, with attention paid to the regularity and frequency with which it is updated and made universally available. Problems arise when those on irregular or non-standard patterns know, believe or perceive that they are the last to gain access to current information.

Return on investment

Matching work patterns to suit those times when the Website is in greatest usage, and potential and actual customer demands are at their highest, is a key contribution that flexible working makes. Those who manage commercially driven Websites require staff to attend in order to respond directly to orders given over the Web, and to those given by telephone lines as the result of e-dimension information at times suitable to customers.

Part of the strategic management of flexible working, and of the Website itself, must therefore be concerned with assessing peaks and troughs in demand, and ensuring that there are sufficient staff available (see Summary box 4.3).

SUMMARY BOX 4.3: CALL CENTER EXPERIENCES

Lessons in the management of peaks and troughs may be learned from the call center sector. This sector regularly underestimates peak demands especially. Because of the physical nature of the act of making a telephone call, customers can be put in a queue and their case dealt with on a first come, first served basis. This is behaviorally and culturally institutionalized.

The Web is much less so. Patterns of behavior in response to Web glitches and shortcomings are much less orderly and predictable, and much more volatile. Customers have a much greater propensity to abandon their attempts to conduct business over the Web immediately if it becomes known or perceived to be inconvenient. They also appear to have a much lower tolerance level of inadequacies compared with telephone and face-to-face conduct of activities.

Source: "Management development in call centres," *Management Today*, May 2000.

Another part of strategic management in fitting work patterns to Website demand must address quality of working life as part of the e-dimension investment. Conducted in isolation and without reference to the environment, e-work becomes as meaningless and alienating as the factory or production line operations during the first Industrial Revolution. This form of working requires the same attention to the environment as every other form of activity.

Return on investment must also be concerned with wider questions of what the e-dimension is adding to the total value of operations and activities – and what is being diluted or damaged if the Website is not fully effective. This reinforces the need for input from the staff who operate it, and its derived activities, when it is up and running, and for staff training and development in efficient and effective operational practices.

CONCLUSIONS

The effectiveness of the e-dimension as a contribution to flexible working is therefore clearly dependent on the quality of the strategic assessment of its likely and possible contribution to total organization performance, the extent to which it is possible to meet this, and then designing patterns of work and working hours in support of it.

Those who carry out the work require training and development to ensure that the opportunities inherent are maximized, and that operating problems are raised and resolved early. From the staff point of view, effectiveness is enhanced or diluted by the attention given to the universality of quality and access to information whatever the hours or patterns of work. Failure to do so is certain to result in feelings of isolation and alienation, and this is a key management priority in designing and implementing effective flexible working (see also Chapters 6 and 8).

KEY LEARNING POINTS

» The true effectiveness of the e-dimension in contributing to flexible working is not yet fully realized or universal.
» Recognize the importance and value of communications, and the contribution of e-mail and electronic information systems.
» Attention must be paid to the operational aspects of Websites.
» There is a potential relationship between technology and increased workloads.
» Technology is of use only in support of effective product and service delivery, and in helping to manage effective flexible working.
» There is a need for a return on the investment.

BEST PRACTICE CASE: FLEXIBLE WORKING AT THE MANAGEMENT STUDIES CENTRE OF UNIVERSITY COLLEGE LONDON

University College London (UCL) was founded in 1843. For the whole of its existence it has had an enduring reputation for high-quality teaching and research excellence, especially in the areas of engineering, physics, archaeology and architecture. More recently, it has developed a reputation for excellence in the fields of law, history and languages, and this last has been reinforced by its takeover, in 1999, of the University of London's School of Oriental and African Studies, and the School for Slavonic and Eastern European Studies.

In 1995, UCL opened its Management Studies Centre. It was designed and created by

» Chris Pitt, Professor of Electrical Engineering

» Graham Winch, now Professor of Management Economics, University of Manchester Institute of Science and Technology
» Andrew Scott, senior lecturer in Physical Sciences, and
» Helen Butcher, Director of Programs, School of Library, Archive and Information Studies.

It was to have two primary purposes:

» to develop a range of undergraduate programs of study with in-built management elements (e.g. engineering with management; statistics with management; information management; French with management); and
» to build on the fledgling and *ad hoc* approaches to management teaching that were being undertaken in other faculties (e.g. construction management, psychology) according to the expertise and interest of specific members of staff.

Because of the engineering and building tradition, the Management Studies Centre placed a strong emphasis on project management. Because of the already crowded teaching timetable, it was resolved that classes would be institutionalized on Tuesday and Thursday afternoons (this was subsequently extended to Fridays).

Many of the staff engaged were part-time. The reasoning behind this was to ensure the best possible mix between teaching excellence and currency of practice.

At inception, it quickly became apparent that, while the structure was sound, much of the support for students was *ad hoc* and dependent entirely on staff location and willingness to attend at other times, or to give out home and business phone numbers.

When the UCL Website and intranet were developed in 1996/7, the Management Studies Centre became the first UCL department to insist that all students had Website access and an e-mail address. This was to ensure that the strengths inherent in the situation could be built on and developed through the virtual medium. The fundamental soundness and freshness of the approach, and high quality of teaching, would therefore be complemented by:

- the availability of virtual access to any member of staff at all times of the day;
- the ability of students and staff to pre-book individual and group tutorials and seminars for the next convenient time (especially Tuesdays and Thursdays); and
- the ability of those in the department's administrative support to chase up students who had not attended lectures or handed in work.

The immediate consequence was a 40% increase in total enrollments between academic years 1997/8 and 1998/9. While a part of this was explained by enhancing the variety and coverage of programs, extensive staff–student consultation and feedback indicated that the prime consideration of those seeking to attend Management Studies Centre courses was the known and believed extent, quality, value and immediacy of access to staff so that problems and issues were addressed and resolved early.

Of particular value was the e-mail access which allowed students to send drafts of written work and project theses, dissertations and seminar proposals in order to gain early advice, guidance and criticism in advance of meeting up with members of staff or handing in finished pieces of work. Students frequently expressed high levels of satisfaction in the quality of support received, in many cases comparing this favorably with what was available elsewhere in the university under supposed full-time traditional tenured positions, and therefore overtly in a position to offer instant face-to-face support upon request.

Because of the flexible structure built around two immovable pillars (the Tuesday and Thursday teaching timetable), and because the constraints of this were accepted and positively managed, effective attention was institutionalized through the Web, intranet and e-mail systems, and a fully supportive, mutually productive and comprehensively flexible approach to both mainstream work, and individual problems and issues, was achieved.

The Global Dimension of Flexible Working

- » Flexible working approaches to globalization are discussed here under the following headings:
  - » Industrial and public service patterns of work
  - » The travel industry and quality of working life
  - » Manufacturing and production
  - » Academic publishing and product and service development
  - » Organizational opportunities.
- » Best-practice case: Palmair Express.

The global dimension of flexible working is addressed from the following points of view:

» the capability of learning from those organizations and sectors that have been most successful in implementing flexible working in different parts of the world;
» the global opportunities that flexible working offers to multinational and transnational organizations and those that wish to go global;
» the capability to locate in areas of known, believed and perceived strategic advantage in order to secure enduring competitive edges.

This reinforces the view adopted at the start that a key part of effective flexible working is the corporate state of mind and its willingness to look at opportunities from a strategic perspective, and to accept responsibility for pursuing them.

LESSONS IN FLEXIBLE WORKING

The following lessons should be learned from different locations, companies, industries and activities. Each of these brings a different clarity to bear on the whole. Those wishing to engage in effective approaches and practices need to understand that long-term and enduring success requires a full understanding of the total range of opportunities, responsibilities and obligations that each brings.

Industrial and public service patterns of work

Many industries and public services have, for a long time, engaged in flexible working practices.

» *Overtime.* Above all, this was the demand to work overtime as and when required. The approach was universally used during periods of high and nearly full employment of the 1950s and 1960s. It was acceptable because:
  » companies knew that there were continuing and enduring high levels of demand for products and services; and
  » employees could enhance earnings through working additional hours for increased and premium rates of pay.
» *Flexi-time.* This was developed along the lines of:

» core hours in which staff were required to be present (e.g. 10.00 am to 4.00 pm during the day on prescribed days); and

» flexi-hours in which staff would arrange their non-core attendance to suit themselves and their work demands and priorities.

» *Hours to suit.* This was developed alongside the practice of allowing or requiring some staff to work at, or from, home. Those in IT-based occupations (e.g. finance and administrative functions) simply log-on when it suits them. Responsibility for meeting deadlines, delivering work and managing workload remains with the individual. How they arrange their work patterns and balance of working life is their responsibility.

» *Job-and-finish.* This is prevalent in the garment industry where staff are given a volume of work rather than a length of time. When they have completed the volume required for the day/week, they finish. This approach also exists in sales (e.g. volume of calls required), project work (e.g. in IT and engineering, work is scheduled to project completion), and delivery schedules (e.g. in which a volume of deliveries is required by the driver).

» *Twilight hours.* This is where work is scheduled for the hours between 5.00 pm and 11.00 pm (see also Chapter 3).

The universal standard approach of fitting the work to people and fitting people to work has been developed to include demands where they are imposed by:

» the need for maximized and optimized return on investment in technology;

» the need to respond to customers and clients;

» the need to take account of supply side issues; and

» the need for benefit and reputation development that exist alongside (see Fig. 5.1).

The travel industry and quality of working life

Because of the nature of the business, those in the travel industry have to be fully flexible in terms of hours, locations and the "time on, time off" balance. The demands of the job require that prescribed periods of work are subject to delays and cancellations. Those in the industry have to be prepared to work extended hours. They must take the off-duty

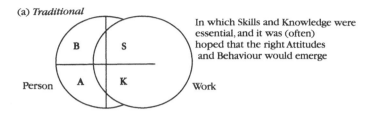

(a) *Traditional*

B   S

Person   A   K   Work

In which Skills and Knowledge were essential, and it was (often) hoped that the right Attitudes and Behaviour would emerge

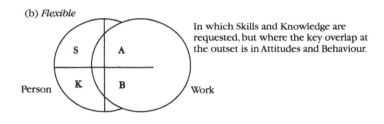

(b) *Flexible*

S   A

Person   K   B   Work

In which Skills and Knowledge are requested, but where the key overlap at the outset is in Attitudes and Behaviour.

S = Skills; **K** = Knowledge; **A** = Attitudes; **B** = Behaviour

Fig. 5.1   Fitting the work to the person and fitting the person to the work.

periods prescribed by the airline, shipping and transport industries, at whichever location they find themselves, when they come off duty.

This brings corporate responsibilities for quality of working life, and the best airlines, shipping and transport companies in-build premium rates of pay and high-quality accommodation arrangements for their staff in different parts of the world (see Summary box 5.1).

SUMMARY BOX 5.1: TIME ON AND TIME OFF

» *British Airways.* The airline engages in corporate arrangements with the Hilton and Movenpick hotel chains so that its pilots, navigation, and cabin crew staff all have guaranteed reservations at these hotels, wherever they are available. If staff are required to take periods of time away from work in locations where these hotels do not have a presence, equivalent accommodation is provided.

» *P&O*. At the beginning and end of each cruise, P&O staff – including ships' officers, catering, sailing and maintenance – are given bonuses to ensure that they are able to pay for 3-, 4- and 5-star accommodation wherever the location may be. At the end of extended periods of duty staff are given bonuses to include extra accommodation if they so desire. They are also provided with free flights to and from pick-up and put-down points.

» *Road haulage*. In the US, the EU and Australia, the best long-distance road haulage companies ensure that their staff have cabs equipped with full domestic facilities; in some cases this includes shower and toilet equipment. Facilities such as television, radio, sleeping accommodation, fridge and microwave oven come as more or less standard.

In all cases, the organizations are doing their best to pay attention to the problems inherent in the particular industry: jetlag; displacement; enclosed or limited environment; working within legal and "best practice" constraints.

They are also trying to ensure that the best possible approach to "a duty of care" is achieved in the circumstances.

Companies in these sectors recognize the disruption to standard and culturally accepted patterns of life. These arrangements substitute a high quality of hotel accommodation and other provisions for the inability to return home at regular intervals and the additional disruptions caused by delays and displacement.

Accordingly, the best companies are able to design, develop and institutionalize predictable patterns of employee behavior, ensuring that:

» professional staff, such as pilots, ships' officers and transport drivers, maintain company loyalty and commitment for the period of a career;

» on-board cabin crew, stewards and catering staff remain for periods of between three and seven years; and

» there is a waiting list of those wanting to work in the industries because of its perceived glamour and independence, and the enhancements given to the life–work balance.

Manufacturing and production

Availability of materials, labor, pressures on costs and the real and perceived high charges for premises in the West have caused those that make and/or sell products to locate or subcontract their manufacturing activities in areas suitable to themselves.

At its most positive, the approach means that the full flexibility of output, market service and product quality is assured. This is reinforced by long-term commitment to the particular communities in the provision of steady streams of employment and other benefits derived as the result of a physical presence. Products required by customers, clients and consumers can be made, distributed and sold anywhere in the world to everyone's mutual advantage. This is, in turn, reinforced by commitment to multi-skilling, initial and continuous job training, assured product and service quality, and absence of demarcation lines, restrictive practices and restraints of trade.

It is necessary to recognize the key aspect of corporate responsibility, however (see also Chapters 2 and 4). The ability to dominate a particular location or sector has led many organizations to subcontract and then dominate and overwhelm their suppliers by driving down the prices that they are willing to pay, and which the suppliers must accept or else find other outlets for their product ranges and volumes. This is not confined to third world garment manufacture (see Summary box 5.2).

SUMMARY BOX 5.2: MARKS & SPENCER: THE SUPPLY SIDE

Historically, Marks & Spencer Ltd, the UK department store chain, built a high-quality enduring reputation for product and service excellence. This was built overwhelmingly on its ability to supply excellent local products and services, using indigenous UK suppliers.

The company first began to dilute this approach with a broader view of its fresh produce suppliers. The company took the view that quality and profit margins could be maintained by dominating indigenous producers of fruit and vegetables, and then driving down the prices that they were willing to pay. This led to unilateral contract cancellations as the company found alternative suppliers on the mainland of Europe.

The company persisted with its policy of buying its clothing from local producers until the year 2000. In November of that year, it unilaterally cancelled the contracts with three large manufacturers in the lowlands of Scotland. The company announced that, in common with many other garment retailers, it was going to concentrate its sourcing in the third world. Overnight, 4500 jobs were lost. The accompanying bad publicity contributed further to decline in organization performance.

In 1998, Marcus Sieff, the last of the descendants of the company's founders, retired from the board of directors. For many analysts, the company's decline in performance can be traced to this incident. It is also possible to draw a direct relationship between the dilution of the company's absolute commitment to local sourcing and high-value work on the supply side, to its loss of distinctive reputation among its customers.

It is also true that flexibility without responsibility requires sustained corporate expenditure on brand building and public relations in order to offset the negative publicity that otherwise tends to accrue (see Summary box 5.3).

SUMMARY BOX 5.3: NIKE

Nike, the US sports and leisurewear company, started to receive large volumes of customer complaints about a particular brand of children's tracksuit. The stitching was found to be faulty and the garments were coming apart, either through normal usage, or else in their first wash.

The company accordingly issued a statement greatly regretting the occurrence, and promising a no-quibble, full refund regardless of whether customers could produce receipts or not.

The company was universally praised for its high moral stance and attention to customer satisfaction. In fact, the entire effort was concentrated on the perceived high-quality customer relations and attention to customer satisfaction on the part of the company. Additionally, nobody went to the factories in Vietnam and Laos where the garments had been made to see what the consequences were on that side.

Academic publishing and product and service development

In 1992, Benjamin Cummings Inc., the US nursing and medical studies publisher, began selling its books with enclosed CD-ROM supporting material. This enabled students to engage in interactive exercises and manipulate diagrams and information in support of their studies in their own time, away from the college and tutors.

This approach spread to other academic publishers and disciplines. As the World Wide Web became more or less universally available, so did the demand for Internet support, downloads, additional material and book updates. This had at least two consequences.

» Publishers needed to develop skills, knowledge and expertise in Website design.
» Authors became required to take a much more active and flexible attitude to the ways in which their expertise was to be presented to the world, and to recognize that global, rather than parochial or direct experienced-based, material was necessary.

The approach also spread to other areas of publishing, including the following.

» Stephen King experimented in publishing a novel chapter by chapter that could only be downloaded from the Internet. A master of his craft, he nevertheless had limited initial success because the public

were used to buying books rather than switching on the computer
and downloading the material chapter by chapter.

» There were treasure hunts, in which books were sold on the basis
that, by following a series of instructions and travelling to both
physical and Website locations, prizes and rewards were gained.

» There developed a published/virtual mix, so that people could either
buy the physical product, or download only the parts that they
wanted (as with the titles in this ExpressExec series).

This emphasizes the relationship between flexibility, creativity and
product and service advancement. It is based on the capability and willingness of both organizations and those who work for them to pursue
a combination of media, technology and expertise, and to develop
the skills, knowledge and attitudes thus required. It also reinforces
the concept of flexibility as a corporate, collective, professional and
occupational attitude.

ORGANIZATIONAL OPPORTUNITIES

As well as drawing lessons in effective flexible working from the world,
there are opportunities that become apparent for many organizations
provided that there is a corporate attitude and willingness to recognize
and develop them.

So much technology is portable that anything that is computer-,
information- or Website-based can be delivered anywhere. This includes
professional services and expertise; all forms of consultancy; and core
training and development material. It also means that those working in
different parts of the world can refer instantly back to headquarters for
decisions and advice when required.

It has also enabled organizations to locate technology-based operations wherever it suits. For example, the world's largest credit card
processing center is in Bombay, India, and this manages billions of
transactions conducted on behalf of US and EU finance and credit card
companies.

Again, however, the key is corporate responsibility and respect for
local culture and social priorities, as well as the opportunities overtly
afforded by the drive for development in the third world and former
Communist bloc.

CONCLUSIONS

Lessons in flexible working can be learned from all sectors in all parts of the world. Whatever the approach taken, however, it is essential that an understanding be achieved of the critical elements of the work and the skills, knowledge, attributes, qualities, attitudes, behavior and expertise. This requires an understanding of the kind of people who are likely to hold these qualities. It requires an understanding of the extremes of the job:

» those elements that are brilliant and attractive, and that consequently attract applications from people who wish only to carry out those parts of it;

» those elements that are boring, dirty and dangerous; and

» those elements that require personal displacement (for example, working away from home for long periods of time).

Each of the lessons mentioned above indicates the need to produce effective work definitions, so that people who are both capable and willing to carry it out can be drawn into it. From a management point of view, therefore, the main quality necessary is recognition of the value of the work. This represents the first and most important step in the structuring of flexible, dynamic and responsive workforces and work practices.

If these lessons are not learned, then the initial premise on which flexible work is structured is flawed; and if this occurs, then the overall effects are always diluted.

KEY LEARNING POINTS

» The corporate approach is required.

» There are implications to particular patterns of work.

» Flexibility needs to accommodate the mix and match of people, work, and demands.

» There is a need for absolute standards.

» There is potential for using creative drives in the pursuit of more effective work patterns.

» Portable technology has a part to play.

BEST PRACTICE CASE: PALMAIR EXPRESS: FLEXIBILITY, QUALITY, PRODUCTIVITY AND PROFITABILITY

Palmair Express has just one aircraft and its 73-year old chairman waves off every flight. Despite its diminutive size and less than extensive schedule, the airline – based at Bournemouth Airport, UK – has put international air travel giants to shame.

It was voted third best airline in the world in a survey of 31,000 passengers conducted by the UK Consumers Association. It was narrowly beaten by Air New Zealand and Singapore Airlines; however, the company left other British carriers, including British Airways and Virgin Atlantic, far behind. Palmair's third place compares with Virgin Atlantic at ninth and British Airways at twenty-sixth, in the list of 50 international airlines.

The chairman, Peter Bath, greets every passenger. His airline, which employs 22 cabin crew, operates 14 flights a week mainly to European destinations.

Mr Bath, who founded the airline in 1957, was thrilled to receive the Consumers Association award. He said:

"After more than 40 years getting up early six mornings a week to greet departing passengers, it is second nature to me. We get a massive amount of repeat business and people get to know our staff. It is a bit like a family gathering. We are delighted and stunned to be so highly regarded."

The survey asked passengers whether they would recommend the airline to a friend. Respondents were also asked to rate each airline according to cabin air supply, crew, catering, check-in staff, cleanliness, entertainment, leg room, seat allocation, seat comfort, lavatories, washrooms, and value for money.

The company recently switched from a BAE146 Whisperjet to a Boeing 737. It increased its passenger numbers from 38,000 to 50,000 per year. The company offers weekly flights to destinations that include Portugal, Greece, Spain, the Canary Islands and Croatia.

The company's managing director is David Skillicorn. He said:

"We removed a row of seats from the plane to give people more leg-room. Customer comfort is very important to us. We have always offered seating allocation as part of the service whereas some airlines charge for it."

The twenty female and two male cabin crew were all recruited and trained by Palmair Express. Mr Skillicorn states:

"We have a range of ages across the board from 19 up to 50, and two are 49 years old. The older cabin crew members have an amalgam of experience from other carriers such as BA. This means we have been able to create our own way of doing things, using the best practice from all the different areas of experience that our crews have. We have developed our own style, though it is not as flamboyant as it was in earlier times."

The company depends for its enduring success on the relationship between the following:

» high-quality, well-paid, highly motivated staff;
» concentration of everything on customer service and flight reliability;
» high and enduring levels of customer loyalty because people have to be prepared to arrange their own schedules around the constraints of a UK regional airport, rather than going to Heathrow or Gatwick;
» attendance to continuous product and service development, including airport facilities, the quality of in-flight food and comfort; and
» a staff development program that includes attention to personal commitment and capability, as well as professional and occupational proficiency.

The State of the Art

» Hours and patterns of work must be regular enough to ensure continuity rather than fragmentation so that quality and value can be engaged and achieved.

» The creation of truly effective flexible skills, knowledge, attitudes, behavior and output requirements transcend any extent of statutory protection or labor market freedom.

» The relationship between pay and performance has never been fully developed. In flexible working, the drive is to reflect staff collective and individual perceptions of the expectation, effort and reward balance, as well as organizational requirements of high-quality, high-value work – for which high levels of pay and reward are expected to accrue.

» Attempts to tie in pay rates with organizational profitability must be applied on the fundamental basis of equality. Pay and other material benefits (e.g. stock option schemes) must be available to all.

» Owing to advances in technology, competitiveness, and structural and cultural pressures, the "portable career" has come about, as well as casualization and alternative forms of employment.

» The life-work balance must suit both individuals and the organizations that employ them.

Effective flexible working is based on combining the principles indicated in previous chapters (and learning from the experience of those who have implemented them), with the organizational, strategic and operational context in which activities are to be carried out. This, in turn, gives rise to a series of principles of implementation and management which are required to ensure that, whatever the design of work, patterns of attendance and nature of operations and activities, effectiveness, success and profitable organizational and individual performance are achieved.

HOURS AND PATTERNS OF WORK

These must be regular enough to ensure continuity rather than fragmentation so that quality and value can be engaged and achieved. Those on irregular hours need the following conditions:

» individual periods of attendance to be long enough to develop a positive identity with the organization and colleagues, and knowledge and understanding of the prevailing context, demands and output requirements; and
» individual periods of attendance to be frequent enough to maintain general familiarity rather than having to be effectively re-inducted on each occasion.

Those working away from the office for long periods – for example, field sales and consultancy teams – are best managed if this is understood. On those occasions when they do attend at the office, it is essential that periods for social interaction be in-built, together with work-oriented meetings, so that personal, as well as professional and occupational, confidence and identity are enhanced.

Those who work away from headquarters for long periods, and whose attendance is intermittent, require managerial and supervisory support based on an openness of relationship, regular periods in which the manager "manages by walking around" – visiting off-site and field staff on a regular basis (Mark McCormack of IMG always rings each of his field staff at least once a week). Staff working in these situations also require continuing flows of high-quality information and other support so that the relationship is enhanced and assured despite the constraints of the work patterns.

This also applies to those on extended hours. Effective working for long hours is possible only where there is a clear goal at the end, or for short concentrated periods. This is a direct contradiction of the practice of many US, UK and Japanese public service and multinational corporations which require long periods of extended hours attendance as a mark of loyalty and commitment (see Summary box 6.1).

SUMMARY BOX 6.1: *KAROUSHI*

Following the devastation of World War II, the Japanese worked extremely hard to rebuild their country and create a successful industrial power. At the core of this turnaround is an enduring level of extremely hard work on the part of its people. For example, the average American spends about 1600 hours per year at work; however, the comparable figure for Japan is 2150 hours. For some Japanese people working long periods without time off is not unusual, in some cases, up to 50 days without a break. This exceptionally hard work comes at a cost. For an increasing number of Japanese people this has led to tragedy.

The Japanese call this *karoushi* which translates as "sudden death from overwork." In one case, an employee of a building company worked 135 hours of overtime a month before he collapsed. Some nights he slept in his Tokyo office, rather than spending the two hours required to return to his home in Osaka.

One expert, Dr Walter Tubbs, has argued that this is not simply overwork that is killing these Japanese workers, but overwork *"combined with feelings of depression and helplessness."* He prefers to think of *karoushi* as "stress death" because its victims not only worked very hard, but were forced to endure additional sources of stress, especially the need to provide a high and improving standard of living for families. Many of the victims studied by Tubbs appear to have been in jobs in which they had minimal control and influence. Those affected were caught up in a cycle in which they were required to work long hours at undesirable jobs in order to secure the standard of living to which they aspired. It is the resulting feelings of helplessness and powerlessness that causes death, rather than the long hours themselves, and the physical and mental exhaustion.

Corporate responsibility and necessary culture change are required to address the following.

» *The attitude that these attendance patterns are productive.* They are not. In the West, business performance decline at IBM (US), BT (UK) and Air France (France) can all be traced to the period when long hours attendance was a cultural, as well as managerial, norm.

» *Rewarding people with bonuses for engaging in this form of attendance.* Again, the problem can be traced to US and UK multinational organizations (as well as Japanese) which effectively paid rewards for attendance largely because they did not otherwise know how to measure managerial and executive performance.

Sources: Tubbs, W. (1993) "*Karoushi*: stress death and the meaning of work," *Journal of Business Ethics*; and Greenberg, J. & Baron, R. (1998) *Behavior in Organizations: Understanding and Managing the Human Side of Work*. Prentice Hall International.

CONTRACTS AND CONDITIONS OF EMPLOYMENT

In the EU there are substantial statutory protections that apply to all staff regardless of length of service or hours worked. In Japan and Korea there are corporate stigmata attached to the commitment to provide employment for life and security of tenure; to fail to do so brings shame on the organization and its top managers. In the US and other parts of the world, labor markets are largely unregulated.

However, as stated in Chapter 3, the creation of truly effective flexible skills, knowledge, attitudes, behavior and output requirements transcend any extent of statutory protection or labor market freedom. To be fully effective, regardless of length of service, patterns of attendance or hours of work, employees require:

» known, believed and perceived confidence that continuity of work and security of employment is assured provided that they do a good job and the organization continues to perform;

» knowledge and belief that their expertise is valued and respected by the organization;

» the belief that, if they are prepared and willing to be flexible at short notice, then they will be consulted with and engaged in decision-making processes (where again, there are statutory obligations in the member states of the EU);

» to be treated on the same fundamental basis of equality in terms of opportunity, demeanor, reporting relationships, management and supervisory style, attendance to security, and opportunities for training, development, enhancement and advancement; and

» to be paid and rewarded on the same fundamental basis also.

PAY AND REWARDS

The relationship between pay and performance has never been fully developed. In flexible working, the drive is to reflect the following:

» staff collective and individual perceptions of the expectation, effort and reward balance (see Fig. 6.1); and

» organizational requirements of high-quality, high-value work – for which high levels of pay and reward are expected to accrue (see Summary box 6.2).

SUMMARY BOX 6.2: HIGH-QUALITY, HIGH-VALUE WORK AND REWARDS

There is a proverb made popular in Hungary during the communist period: *"We pretend to work, and they pretend to pay us."*

This reflects low-value, low-quality work, for low levels of reward – and low levels of intrinsic respect and esteem. Because each element was in harmony, there was no overt strain provided that the low levels of reward could sustain a certain standard of living and quality of life.

(a) *Simple*

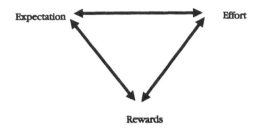

(b) *Complex*

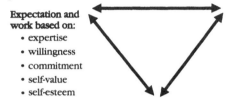

Fig. 6.1 The work/quality/rewards equation.

Institutional problems arise when the relationship is skewed as follows.

» *High quality, high value, low reward* – possible in the short term; possible when there is scarcity of work; leads always to frustration.

» *Low quality, high value, low reward* – possible in the short term only.

> *High quality, low value, high reward* – standard efficiency rather than effectiveness; normally means that the organization is procedure driven, rather than customer or product/service driven.
> *Low quality, low value, high reward* – the equivalent of over-paying and is wasteful; is normally sustainable only in the short term or where there is an enduring captive market.

Corporate and strategic decisions are required on the mix to be achieved. If anything other than high quality/high value/high reward is contemplated, then the consequences must be clearly understood.

PROFIT-RELATED PAY

All attempts to tie in pay rates with organizational profitability must be applied on the fundamental basis of equality; pay and other mate-rial benefits (e.g. stock option schemes) must be available to all. The purpose is to reward effective efforts, rather than penalize them. Effec-tive profit and performance-related pay ensures that all staff concentrate on the purposes for which they are supposed to be working, and that they take a positive stake in operational success.

The profit-related elements must include the allocation of percent-ages, proportions or amounts from the surpluses generated by the organization to the staff; and the means by which this is to be allocated should also be made clear in advance of any actual reward, in the inter-ests of both fairness, and also confidence in the scheme. Organizations that offer stock options and equity to build staff commitment, public confidence and the market value of the organization should also be available for universal inspection. Organizations that offer cash bonuses must ensure that these are distributed on an equitable basis; this is often best achieved through giving everyone an equal percentage of their annual salary.

In general, the following conditions are required.

> The profit-related pay schemes must be believed in, valued and understood by all concerned.

» Any targets set must be achievable; these must neither be too easy nor too difficult. Their purpose is to balance effective effort and output.
» The aim is to reward effort and achievement on the part of all staff whatever their role or occupation.

All pay and reward strategies must address the following:

» staff, professional and occupational expectations;
» motivation and incentives over immediate, and also enduring, periods of time;
» allowances as and when required, paid, for example, for disturbance, shift, weekend, unsocial hours, training and development, location and relocation, and absence from home; and
» economic rent – high rates of pay for particular expertise (especially scarce expertise or that which is required at short notice).

Organizations must therefore understand what they are paying for, and why, and the consequences of different attitudes and approaches. In general, when paying for flexible expertise, skills, knowledge, attitudes and technological proficiency, high levels of pay and rewards, and other opportunities, must be present if an enduring profitable relationship is required. Low pay for high-quality work is sustainable only in the short term, or if it rises steeply after an initial trial period (see Summary box 6.3).

SUMMARY BOX 6.3: NURSING IN THE UK

The nursing profession in the UK is suffering the consequences of generations of undervalue. Low pay for high-value and high-quality work has led to staff shortages, an aging professional workforce, and the inability to recruit and retain newcomers to the profession.

In this, and in all other such cases, the only solution is to raise the pay to levels commensurate with the quality of work and professional and personal commitment required.

Nothing else will do in the long term. All organizations that manage to employ staff on low pay in return for high-quality, high-value work will retain them only until opportunities become available elsewhere.

This attitude to work is an extreme mark of low respect and value, and jobholders understand this as such.

CAREER AND WORK PATTERNS

Long-term, steady-state careers in organizations, professions and occupations are no longer possible. Owing to advances in technology, competitiveness, and structural and cultural pressures that arise as the result, the portable career has come about.

The portable career

This has the following elements:

» a collective and, above all, personal responsibility and commitment to develop the range of skills, knowledge, attitudes, behavior and expertise necessary to remain employable; and
» the willingness and capability to develop expertise in existing professions and occupations.

This requires taking an active personal interest in the latest thinking, practice, technological and professional advances in all jobs and occupations. This is leading to a much broader conception of continuous professional and occupational development. Such an attitude was originally required only in those who aspired to genuinely "professional" status – especially medicine and the law. It is presently required of anyone who seeks to remain and be effective in any functional specialization.

The same attitudes are required in those without the same degree of known or perceived expertise. Those formerly classified as "unskilled" now require flexible and positive attitudes to whatever opportunities come their way. Much of the transformation in mass production and mass occupation sectors has been socially and culturally traumatic, as those who hitherto worked in these areas have experienced job and economic losses without, in many cases, having anything to replace it. The problems have been alleviated in part when new organizations have replaced the old. In many cases, however, this has meant expectational, as well as social and cultural, shifts because communities previously based on, for example, mining, engineering or shipyards have had to get used to engaging in retail, service and assembly work.

The combination of each of these elements means that people are going to need and require to change employer, occupation and work emphasis at different times over their working lives. They are increasingly likely to have to get used to variable, rather than assured, levels of income. This has implications for house purchase, medical assurance and pension and retirement arrangements. This, in turn, has led to insistence by those who are able to do so, of assured current high levels of pay to build up both security and resources for times when earnings may be less certain.

Casualization

The other side of the portable career is the great increase in the volume and nature of work being subject to casualization in which:

» employers take on staff on the basis that they will be engaged only for periods in which there is work to be carried out; and
» employees accept work on the basis that there is no guarantee of long-term or enduring work.

Other forms of employment

Other forms include engaging people on temporary, fixed-term or seasonal contracts and arrangements to cope with peaks in demand and sudden staff shortages among the core workforce. Originally almost exclusively confined to office, building and factory work, it is now found in public service, health and social care, education, sales and "new industries" such as call centers, telecommunications, dotcom and catering work.

The perceived advantage to organizations is the lack of institutional and enduring commitment to what would otherwise be a full-time established workforce. This has to be balanced against the increasingly (and understandable) mercenary attitude of those in short-term or casualized work and the consequent loss or dilution of mutuality of identity, interest and commitment, and any effects that each of these may bring to long-term organizational effectiveness.

Both casualization and the use of agencies are, superficially, extremely attractive to media analysts and stock markets. This is because, as these forms of employment increase, then full-time equivalent headcount decreases and this is attractive to many brokers dealing with different sectors in various parts of the world (see Summary box 6.4).

SUMMARY BOX 6.4: BUSINESS PROCESS RE-ENGINEERING CONSULTANTS

Many of the world's top brand management consultants (including McKinsey, Booz Allen Hamilton, and Ernst & Young) engaged in restructuring and downsizing programs by assuring the financial interest of the contracting organization that they would benefit from immediate share value gains provided that they were allowed to reduce the payroll to a certain size, or a certain percentage, of capital value or gross turnover.

This approach was developed to such an extent that, by the end of the twentieth century, share values were being enhanced merely by the knowledge that one of the big consulting firms had been engaged.

Almost without exception, the short-term advantage was not sustained. The overriding reason was that the consultants paid insufficient attention to the management priorities and staffing considerations and requirements of the new restructured – and reduced – workforce.

Effective casualization and use of temporary staff requires attention to the enduring volume and quality of work required and the nature of the casualized or subcontracted working relationship so that everyone's interests are satisfied. Failure to do this means that, given any choice in the matter, staff will go to work for those organizations where a greater value and expectation is placed on their flexibility and positive attitudes, as well as their availability.

LIFE–WORK BALANCE

The capability of individuals

This involves the capability of individuals to arrange their working hours around other commitments, as well as the willingness of employers to accept that employees have other commitments.

One part of the development of flexible working has concerned zero hours in which employees are requested to work as and when required with no minimum hours or specific guarantees of work. Another concerns annualized hours that can then be arranged and agreed between employee and employer, and other commitments worked in around it.

The capability of organizations

Organizations in some parts of the world offer sabbaticals or extended periods of leave; at the end of each, the ability to return to work is assured. The practice is popular in Australia, New Zealand and South Africa and is seen as a key element of the retention package.

It also involves the capability and willingness of organizations to contribute to the wider social fabric and development of the locations in which they exist and operate. This means:

» willingness to sponsor local social events, facilities, sports, leisure and recreation clubs;
» willingness to put resources into local schools, hospitals and social services; and
» openness and commitment to the community at large, as well to those who are directly employed.

This is, above all, a development of corporate attitudes away from the narrow pursuit of profit. It involves accepting the place of common humanity and decency as a key feature of corporate life; and in most cases, it contributes to profitability because people are prepared and willing to deal with organizations that adopt these values.

Other businesses take the view that they will contract out specialist services and other short-term requirements to local providers only, or at least give them the first opportunity to produce.

Each of these elements combines to form and develop a much broader and more flexible and positive attitude as to what contributes to long-term enduring effectiveness and viability (see Summary box 6.5).

SUMMARY BOX 6.5: CAPTIVE CUSTOMERS

A variation of the life–work approach was conducted in central Scotland in late 2000 and early 2001. A survey of the leading employers of the central industrial belt, comprising Glasgow, Edinburgh, and "the silicon glen" at Dunfermline, revealed initially that 92% of customers and clients were happy with the products and services available from organizations in these places.

However, when follow-up work was carried out in which the same customers and clients were asked "Given any choice in the matter, would you change providers?", 75% of respondents said they would. The reasons given were

inflexible attitudes
unwillingness to listen
poor after-sales service and complaint handling
high levels of charges.

The overwhelming conclusion was that, while the organizations were by no means the worst in the world, they were able to exist at present levels of profitability only because of the largely local captive markets and the lack of real choices available.

Source: Cartwright, R. (2000) *Mastering Customer Relations*. Macmillan Palgrave.

There is also an ethical and wholesome element in the life–work balance. If organizations genuinely recognize the value placed by employees on life outside work, then:

» they can concentrate quite legitimately on the quality of performance while at work; and
» they can integrate their expectations with those of employees much more effectively.

The working relationship is therefore developed from the point of view of mutual understanding and coincidence of interest, rather than creating the stresses and strains that are universally present when the work and non-work parts of life clash (see Summary box 6.6).

SUMMARY BOX 6.6: KEEPING A HAPPY SHIP

Working times and practices have a much wider impact on society than the business or company that dictates them. Working culture also impacts upon society at large.

A whole generation grew up in the 1980s not seeing their parents, who spent their lives in the office instead of at home. The UK historically suffered from a productivity problem and it may be that some managers are finally beginning to realize why.

Most people spend close to the majority of their waking hours in the workplace. Consequently, in order for everyone to maintain a happy disposition they must enjoy at least some of that time. Workplaces do not have to be austere environments, and people should not have to be there for longer than is necessary. It is also not necessary to have bad relationships with bosses. Humor, motivation and sensible hours are keys to present working environments and logical to increase productivity for all.

Many chief executives are beginning to appreciate the idea that creating a more human environment in the workplace and allowing staff to keep sensible hours could be beneficial for all concerned. A survey by Office Angels Inc. revealed that more than 75% of human resource directors believe that motivated and happy workers increase their respective company's profits. The problem is that only 18% felt their companies were actively encouraging such environments.

A key problem is that many organizations do not yet know how to create more friendly, relaxed or happy working environments. Part of the problem lies in the fact that many of those in senior management positions had to struggle up the career ladder during periods of high unemployment and organizational restructuring and downsizing. Ultimately, however, the hard slog of long working days in austere environments creates little benefit for anyone. Workers who convince themselves that putting in long hours today will reap rewards for the future are likely to be wasting their time. Many managers recognize that working long hours for the sake of it brings few benefits. Because individuals stay late at the place of work, this does not necessarily mean that they are working harder. Tired and demotivated, staff do not increase their productivity by putting in more hours. Shorter, but highly productive, days are clearly more beneficial for all concerned.

Attention to the life-work balance involves creating the right kind of environment, attention to hours of work, and management style. If this is achieved, costs are reduced through reduced staff turnover and increased attendance. This, in turn, reduces the stresses and strains placed on those staff who do remain in the organization.

Sources: Office Angels Inc. (2000) *Quality of Working Life*. Deloitte and Tousche; and Ledger, W. (1998) "Keeping a happy ship," *London Evening Standard*.

CONCLUSIONS

Effective flexible working concerns attention to the combination of:

» patterns of work and expertise available;
» organizational demands;
» the need for returns on investment;
» customer and client demands;
» attention to the life-work balance and the ability to take an enlightened view of this.

Each of these elements requires understanding and acceptance by the top managers of organizations as a prerequisite to their effective integration into the development and implementation of proposed strategy, policy, priorities and direction. Above all, it is necessary to pay attention to the value and quality of work required, and the conditions necessary to ensure that this is present, and capable of achievement.

It must be recognized that the creation and implementation of flexible work patterns is required to ensure that the organization maximizes and optimizes its potential over the long term, and that customers and clients receive enduringly excellent levels of products and services whenever these are required.

KEY LEARNING POINTS

It is important to understand:

» the opportunities available through the use of different hours of work and patterns of attendance;

» the complexity of structuring different patterns of work into an integrated organizational whole;

» staff expectations – especially the drive for increased immediate rewards because of the nature of occupational turbulence and uncertainty;

» the direct balance between high-value, high-quality work and the need for high levels of reward – and the consequences of failing to address one or more of these;

» the concept of the portable career, and the opportunities and constraints around employing those who work on non-standard patterns of work, through agencies, and on casual bases;

» the implications of the life–work balance in particular situations.

Flexible Working Success Stories

The chapter looks at the following case studies:

- » Sandals Inc.
- » British Airways
- » Cobra Beer
- » Semco Inc.

Each of the examples in this chapter illustrates the contribution made by the adoption of flexible working policies and approaches to enduring corporate success. The need for a strategic perspective is reinforced. It is also essential to recognize that attention to every detail is required if the whole is to be fully effective in the long term. The examples are:

» Sandals Inc. – continued attention to developing the highest possible levels of customer satisfaction in a top brand leisure organization;
» British Airways – the contribution of the company's new head office to culture, transformation, business development, and reprioritization of working practices and attitudes;
» Cobra Beer – flexible attitudes, approaches, marketing, and working practices in developing commercial advantages across frontiers; and
» Semco – flexible working as a catalyst for change.

SANDALS INC.

Sandals Inc. provides top-quality holiday accommodation and leisure services in the West Indies. The target market is couples from the US, the UK, the EU; marketing promotion and presentation are targeted at those who have a joint disposable income of between $70,000 and $100,000 per annum.

Each resort is individually designed. The company describes these as follows.

"Tropical hideaways on the beautiful Caribbean Islands of Antigua, St. Lucia, Jamaica and The Bahamas, where you will be pampered morning, noon and night – and it is all included in one up-front price.

"Where superb delicacies are complements of the chef and top brand named drinks are on the house for the entire length of your holiday – this is the world of Sandals ultra all-inclusive resorts. And if you want to take other family members with you, don't despair, because Sandals has created Beaches – five ultra all-inclusive resorts on Jamaica, Cuba and the Turks and Caicos Islands that cater for everybody – singles, couples, families and friends.

"The experience is the same – luxurious accommodation, fabulous gourmet meals, any time snacks, land and water-based sports, professional instruction, even tipping – it is all in one easy all-inclusive price.

"Your holiday means as much to us as it means to you. So when you book with the company, you are assured of a caring, highly personal service."

Distinctive standards

In 1996, Elaine Vaughan was appointed managing director and chief executive officer. Her key contribution was to ensure that everyone in the company was enthused with the same ambition, commitment and energy that she herself brought.

Accordingly, promotional and presentational materials were redesigned, and the target market identified. Staff were placed on immediately enhanced terms and conditions of employment to reflect the increasing level of demand that would now be placed on them. The company undertook to pay at least 50% above local minimum prescribed rates of pay. In return, staff were engaged in fully flexible training programs, including customer service, bar, food and environment management, and in the levels of responsiveness that guests from the US and EU would require in return for paying the levels of prices charged. Vaughan stated:

> "We are selling people's dreams. This is the best job in the world. We must make sure that their dreams are not just met, but exceeded. If we do not do this, people will simply go elsewhere. So everything has to be right – and this, above all, means the staff. If we put something on, it is the staff who deliver it. So I want everybody – me included – to understand that everything that they do contributes to customer service, and to be trained accordingly. The customers must never ever be turned away."

Weddings

A key feature of the Sandals offering is "the wedding package." This is offered in two forms.

The free "wedding-moon" package

This includes:

preparation of documentation
copies of marriage licenses and legal fees
marriage certificates
ceremony officiant
wedding reception within a beautifully decorated area
taped musical accompaniment
bottle of champagne and hors d'oeuvres
services of personal wedding coordinator
flower bouquet and buttonhole
Caribbean wedding cake
one 5 × 7 inch wedding photograph
honeymoon candlelit dinner for bride and groom
continental breakfast in bed morning after wedding
"Just-married" T-shirts
witnesses if required.

The company also offers to arrange any ceremony at a charge for those wanting a Catholic or other Christian church wedding, weddings of any other religious denomination, and other options. Sandals also provides, at a charge:

a video of the ceremony
hairstyling and make-up sessions
manicures
additional photographic packages
any other special features upon demand.

Weddings in Antigua

Sandals' resort in Antigua is the most preferred destination in the world for wedding and honeymoon couples. For between $8000 and $10,000 per couple, the resort offers a fully inclusive 14-night luxury holiday with wedding and honeymoon arranged to suit.

The company has always had a reputation for high quality in this area of activity. The quality was further transformed as the result of specific initiatives undertaken by the then local CEO, Stephen Garley.

Staff had always been fully flexible in their general attitude to customers following the direction of Elaine Vaughan. Everyone worked extremely hard and for very long hours to ensure maximum satisfaction for the duration of the stay.

Part of the problem with the weddings operation was that staff were almost too flexible. While trying to help couples sort out the elements and features that they wanted for their weddings, staff would constantly be interrupted by other demands, both from wedding and non-wedding guests.

While time and trouble was taken to ensure that weddings were as individual as possible, the context and environment were rigid. Most ceremonies were scheduled to take place on Saturdays and Sundays. The company would try to fit in as many weddings as possible on these days rather than spreading them out over the rest of the week. The consequence was that very often couples were queuing for their ceremony while the previous event was still concluding.

The core wedding package consisted of:

local priest or registrar
bride and bridegroom wear
flowers
photographer and video
champagne, canapes and a wedding cake.

Charges were made for some of these; others were free.

Stephen Garley found that the key immovables were the photographer and video producer. Ceremonies were scheduled for every 30 minutes on Saturdays and Sundays because it suited the providers of these two features – neither of whom worked for the company.

There was also the question of the West Indian environment and the weather. The resort did not provide iced water, despite the fact that the environment was extremely hot. The result of this was that, unless everything went precisely according to timetable, the champagne and canapes would get warm and lose their quality and value in the eyes of the customer. Everybody also got very hot while waiting around. In addition, the islands of the West Indies are subject to constant short sharp showers of rain and there was no provision for slack in the wedding schedule should this happen and delays be required.

There was little coordination between:

» the kitchen, which provided excellent top quality wedding cakes and canapes;
» the bar and cellars, which provided the champagne;
» the wedding coordinator, responsible for each individual wedding and ensuring that the couple, the priest or registrar, the witnesses and the guests all turned up on time, and in the right place; and
» the photographer and video producer.

Flexible work development

Garley accordingly restructured the work to ensure the following.

» Weddings could take place on any day of the week, thereby spreading the workload and avoiding logjams on Saturdays and Sundays.
» The "immovable" linchpins of photographer and video producer were removed by bringing the services in-house and making them available to all those couples who asked for them; and making them available for hire to non-wedding customers also.
» Quiet areas were designated so that staff could deal effectively with wedding customers on an individual basis away from other inquiries. Staff called away for this reason would be covered by colleagues for other general duties.
» Corporate managerial attitudes were developed to ensure that the particular barriers were overcome and to ensure that concentration and focus remained with the customers.

Other actions

» *The environment.* Garley himself took the lead in designing and building two quiet sheltered areas for the weddings. These ensured privacy and a break from the noise from the other guests and activities at the resorts. He ensured that good-quality music provision was laid on, and chiller boxes to keep the food and drinks fresh were provided. Weddings were rescheduled over the course of the week, rather than being packed in to Saturdays and Sundays. Catering, photography and video staff were also included in the proceedings, required to meet and greet the marriage party.

» *Flexible working development.* Local managers were required to reschedule work so that all weddings were fully staffed whatever the time or day of the week. The collective shift was away from resort provision to meeting customer requirements. Both management and wedding coordination staff were required to find out if the couple had any particular requirements, and staff were given leeway to provide additional extras where possible.

» *Work schedules.* Work schedules were prioritized to ensure that full coordination was achieved between kitchen, wedding party officials, photography and video, so that:

   – if there was any time slippage in individual ceremonies, this did not matter;

   – if the wedding party and guests wanted to linger over the post-wedding period, they could; and

   – if the weather suddenly intervened, the food and drinks were not ruined, and staff could remain in attendance.

Conclusions

By reputation, the company already provided the best fully inclusive wedding service in the world. This was not good enough. Accordingly, Sandals was enabled to engage and develop the corporate, collective and individual attitudes to flexible working in order to ensure that this service became of much higher quality, highly polished and customer-oriented, rather than company prescribed. The key to this involved building on the flexible working approaches already present, and ensuring that skills and attitudes were refocused toward customer delight rather than corporate efficiency.

KEY INSIGHTS

» The contribution of effective staff.
» The need for the management of flexible working – however flexible the skills and attitudes, schedules have still to be prioritized and arranged.
» The need for scheduling flexible working skills and attitudes to key groups of customers.

» The need for staff and corporate development and understanding.
» The implementation of collective and individual staff development; the capability to build on flexible skills and attitudes.
» Flexible working not as an end in itself; it has still to be applied effectively to meet the demands of customers and the broader environment.
» The need to address linchpins – known and perceived immovables that prevent the development of fully flexible operations and activities.
» The contribution of a "flexible work champion" – in this case, Stephen Garley.
» The need to relate all employee activities to company and top management vision, policy and direction.
» The need for clear, distinctive and positive standards at the top of the organization.

BRITISH AIRWAYS

Acknowledgment is made to the following sources for information:

» www.BA.co.uk;
» Roffey Park Management Institute UK; and
» Syrett, M. and Lammiman, J. (2000) "Happily landed: British Airways relocation," *People Management* (UK), 28 September.

British Airways' new headquarters

British Airways' reputation for effective change management and staff motivation has taken hefty knocks in the past few years. The costly industrial dispute with the Transport and General Workers Union, the court case against Virgin, and the multimillion pound cost-cutting program, led to a bumpy ride for share prices and tarnished what was once seen as a corporate success story.

Whatever the legacy of these poor years, the company and its former CEO, Bob Ayling, can take justifiable pride in the construction of a business center purpose-built to transform the organization's working practices. It was the largest and fastest construction project of its kind in the UK. It broke new ground in workspace design, facilities management and information technology, as well as creating the conditions and environment in which work, attitudes and priorities could be transformed.

The design features of the Waterside Centre are extraordinary. Set in 113 hectares of landscaped public parkland about a mile from London's Heathrow Airport, six self-contained business modules are enclosed by a glass shell and connected to each other by "The Street," a tree-lined indoor boulevard that offers a supermarket, newsagent, bank, health center, travel office, beauty salon, florist, cafés and restaurants. Work areas on different levels are connected by walkways studded with sofas, easy chairs and coffee tables.

A "no office" culture encourages staff to hold meetings in these public areas. This allows regular informal cross-departmental contact that can spark chance discoveries and innovation. Studies carried out by the company suggest that, at any one time, two-thirds of the users of the central café are engaged in formal or informal business meetings. This has been encouraged by installing computers and telephones near seating areas. These communication points allow staff to log on to computers and conduct video conferences and phone discussions anywhere in the building.

Staff movements have been channeled to maximize use of the communal areas. It is not possible, for example, for people to travel by lift direct from the underground staff car park to their workspace – they have to walk along "The Street."

Each work area is designed to be used like a club. Staff keep papers and equipment in large filing draws and – with the exception of a few key administrators who have their own desks – choose the working area that best suits their needs. Areas closest to the entrances are designed as social points where staff can mix or conduct informal meetings. The middle areas have computer terminals designed either for quick touchdown activities such as checking up on e-mail or diary commitments, or for longer-term activities. In such cases, the space must be booked for a specific time. Private space near windows overlooking the parkland can be reserved for individual work.

The facilities are available not only to the staff based permanently at Waterside, but also to consultants, visitors and temporary workers. The aim was to incorporate working areas to accommodate every possible mode and method of working that could be thought of. The result is a bright modern environment, and a complete contrast to the gloomy corridors of the airline's previous headquarters.

When the project was conceived, the then CEO, Colin Marshall, made it clear that staff in the new headquarters building should be able to "see the planes." Marshall feared that if the administrative and operational staff lost day-to-day contact and visible identity, both strategy and operations would be undermined. This meant that any new building had to be on, or adjacent to, the airport perimeter at Heathrow.

Once the Waterside Centre was constructed, the company's administrative staff, previously housed in 12 locations, were all brought under the one roof. A working environment was designed that encouraged cross-departmental cooperation. The strategic aim was to break down the inert, negative and rank status and hierarchical-driven corporate culture, and replace this with something that served the interests of everybody concerned – above all the passengers who used the airline.

The strategic approach was driven by the human resource management priority – the need to ensure that staff were engaged in effective, flexible and dynamic working practices, and that the new environment would support this.

Returns on investment

The Waterside Centre project cost more than $300mn. The company is now faced with gaining returns on that investment. Straightforward returns – in terms of income/expenditure measures – are clearly not feasible or possible to measure.

Part of the return on this investment has come about through the closure of other offices and the sales or leasing of those premises.

It is clear that returns are also not available in the short term. Airline industry analysts state that, in fact, the company is unable to afford to run these premises on present passenger levels or route network coverage; above all, the company is not a sufficiently dominant player on its key routes to Western Europe and North America to command the premium price levels necessary to gain a one-dimensional return on this investment.

The key is, therefore, to gain a higher return on investment on the staff employed, and a greater quality of production and service on the salary bill. To this extent, contributions are observable, if not quantifiable. Staff surveys show that employees are making full use of the social facilities for business purposes. The facility has the capacity to relocate a further 1500 employees to the building, and this will increase the headcount from 3500 to 5000.

Key contributions

From an HR perspective, the Waterside project is interesting in that almost all the innovations stemmed from the property development. The company's business imperatives prompted the initiatives. Staff management and flexible working breakthroughs occurred because the key managers involved, the general manager Gwilym Rees-Jones and project leader Chris Byron, were persuaded to apply an HR and staff management perspective to what would otherwise have been seen as a constructional property development issue.

The open approach and club concept was developed by facilities manager Alison Hartigan. The purpose was to create a high-quality, comfortable and secure working environment. Based on fundamental principles of equality, this also meant persuading British Airways' directors and senior managers (including the CEO) to give up the right to their own offices.

Conclusions

The conclusion drawn by Chris Byron is as follows.

> "Waterside is a classic example of a people-led strategy. Most of the managers were heavily involved in various aspects of customer service before they transferred, and their sense of the strong relationship between buildings and people was uttermost."

So long as the airline continues to be able to afford to use the facility, there is an excellent basis for effective and fully flexible working at a corporate level.

KEY INSIGHTS
» The need for an effective relationship between the working environment and effective flexible work patterns.
» The need for corporate vision and direction as a key to effective implementation.
» The contribution of individuals, especially Byron, Rees-Jones and Hartigan.
» The need to measure returns on investment; and where these are not clearly visible or apparent, the need to continue the search for effective measures of return on investment.
» The creation of a high-quality working environment so that the organization may demand high levels of output from staff in return.
» The contribution of the collective and club attitudes, and the provision of non-specific working areas, as contributors to developing fully flexible attitudes.
» The behavioral need for visibility of the company's products and services – in this case, the airliners – to ensure that everyone's attention is concentrated on primary purposes.
» The creation of these conditions and attitudes as a precursor to demanding skills, knowledge, attitude and behavior development.

COBRA BEER
Flexible working and product development

Karan Bilimoria is the managing director of Cobra Beer, an Indian brewery that supplies approximately 10% of the beer consumed in Indian restaurants in the UK. The company was founded in Bangalore, India, in 1990. Initially failing to take off in India, Bilimoria turned his attention to the UK market.

The product took off slowly. Its success in gaining a firm initial foothold was entirely down to Bilimoria himself. He traveled from restaurant to restaurant and grocer to grocer to promote the product. It took five years for turnover to hit the $2mn mark. This is now up to $18mn, and revenues grew by 65% over the period 2000–1.

The beer is sold as a combination of:

» a fashion item;
» a necessary and assured accompaniment for Indian food; and
» a branded alternative to indigenous beers and lagers.

The company is now looking to fund expansion, and to develop its markets in the member states of the European Union and the old British Commonwealth. Its key priorities are brand building and establishing the necessary distribution networks.

Strategic initiatives

The company has established a brewery in the UK to supplement the output of that in Bangalore. The company concentrates everything on assuring the quality of product and distribution. Marketing and sales staff are trained to respond instantly to demands for fresh supplies, however small the volume may be.

The company has diversified in grocery store and supermarket sales alongside restaurants. This is to complement the fact that all the major supermarket chains now sell easy-to-prepare and ready-to-eat Indian food. The company has accordingly secured a presence in Tesco, Waitrose and Safeway, three UK supermarket chains.

Staff development

Brewery staff in India and the UK are fully trained in the art of brewing beer. This involves attention to the quality, as well as volume, of ingredients, and absolute standards of cleanliness, hygiene, temperature and environment management. The company has a small hierarchical chain of command only at its Bangalore brewery, and their primary function is to ensure that volumes of product are shipped on time and to the required quantities, wherever in the world they are demanded.

Bilimoria divides his time between the UK and India. He pays particular attention to meeting and understanding the demands, hopes, fears and aspirations of all those who work for him. The company has introduced staff training programs for all. Faced with the prospect of rapid industrial and commercial expansion in India, staff wages and salaries have been raised in order to remain competitive with new industries. Job rotation, flexibility, enhancement and improvements in working conditions and environment have all been introduced.

Bilimoria also continues to develop both his own entrepreneurialism, and also that of his staff. No new idea is ever rejected without debate and discussion, and all employees are encouraged to seek and find new outlets for the product. Staff are rewarded on two counts:

» a commission based on the volume and income generated by the initial sale to the new outlet;
» profit-sharing in the overall annual turnover.

Conclusions

The example of Cobra Beer demonstrates the need for qualities of flexibility, enthusiasm and dynamic in developing a brand, and of gaining both recognition and a commercial foothold in new markets. Bilimoria's own flexible attitude was critical in getting the product launched in the first place; and this has translated into the rest of the staff in all areas of activity. This has, in turn, been supported by extensive staff development programs, driven by the constant need for attention to product quality and customer and consumer convenience.

KEY INSIGHTS

» The relationship between entrepreneurial flare and vision, and flexible working.
» The need for energy and commitment.
» The need for attention to all aspects of product and service development and enhancement.
» The transmission of the attitudes of the company founder into the rest of the staff.
» The relationship between staff development, flexible working and increased competitive edge and advantage.
» Opportunities in niche markets, and the position of flexible working in developing these.
» The need to attend to reward levels so that capability and willingness are recognized and acknowledged.

SEMCO INC.

Flexible working as a catalyst for change

"About this time, I went to Ipiranga to our factory there. Sales of our big industrial dishwashers had dropped from 40 a month, to 25, and then to five. Inventory levels and factory expenses were killing us. If the situation did not improve, I didn't have any doubt, the plant would have to shut."

These were the thoughts of Ricardo Semler, CEO of Semco Inc., as he considered the future of one of his main areas of activity.

He discussed the matter with Joao Soares, then the factory Committee Leader, and now a member of the company's seven-person ruling elite. Soares knew things were bleak but he assured Semler that, provided a flexible and committed attitude was adopted, matters could be turned around. Soares had made huge strides in productivity by engaging fully flexible attitudes, and this would now be a test. If it worked, it would lead to further changes in the direction of full flexibility.

Semler wanted to close the plant. Soares argued that once the present crisis was over, there would be an upturn and it would be necessary to plan for growth. He argued that they had managed the situation without a single lay-off, and this had seen them through crisis. They had managed to cut costs in many areas, and also to maintain productivity so that when the upturn did come, the company would have stocks in hand to be sold. These would generate cash flow and support for future development. Semler listened to the arguments and allowed Soares to have his way.

Soares had risen through Semco from his early life as a street child in Rio de Janeiro. His first job, at the age of nine, was selling peanuts and iced tea at the Maracana soccer stadium in the city. Now his whole life was Semco; this had cost him his marriage.

Entering adulthood, Soares had worked in a succession of factories in which he had never been treated with anything approaching human dignity. At Semco, once he was given responsibility, he had been determined to change everything that he could. He had supported Semler throughout in his approach to transforming Semco from a traditional to a fully flexible organization. They had introduced benefits for all staff: health insurance, free breakfasts, flexible working hours and self-determination for everybody.

The plan

Accordingly, at Ipiranga, Soares gathered all the staff together in the middle of the shop floor. He told them that he had an idea that, if it worked, would save the plant and their jobs. The staff would voluntarily reduce their wages by 30% and forego a 10% pay rise that they were due. They would give up subsidized meals, their transportation allowances and other benefits.

The staff would take over all the services at the plant provided by outside contractors and third parties, and perform them themselves. This would further slash the company's costs. At the cafeteria, the staff would buy the food and prepare it. The staff would guard the factory gates, clean the offices and the workshop when the working day was over. They would transport finished goods to customers and sell replacement parts to restaurants, hotels and offices.

In return, the staff would share with management the authority to run the plant. All business decisions would be made jointly – a guarantee that their sacrifice would not be wasted. All strategies, policies and investments would require approval from both the bosses and the staff. The bosses would consent to a 40% pay cut.

He met initial resistance. Above all, the staff refused to clean the bathrooms. Soares stated that he would be the first to clean the bathrooms. He also said that he would clean the offices. He would ask nothing of anyone that he himself was not prepared to do.

The plan was thrashed through to the point at which it was universally accepted. Those in management positions were not as enthusiastic as the staff and some changes were negotiated. Management accepted the 40% pay cut for two months only, with a 30% reduction thereafter. The cuts were applied in such ways as to ensure that lower paid workers were protected; the greatest cuts would be placed on those at the top of the pay scale. Employees also successfully negotiated an additional profit-sharing payment of 15% of gross profits; this was in addition to the 23% already provided.

The outcome

The results became apparent in the first month. The staff had saved so much that the extra profit-sharing clause was invoked at the end of the first month. The second month was better still; and by the end of the third month, the employees' salaries had been fully restored. Sales of dishwashers rose to 12 a month. The plant also developed its sales of spare parts to the point at which overtime was invoked.

This enabled the company to withstand the recession better than many others in the field. Most of these were forced to lay off about half of their staff. Semco endured a 40% drop in sales and had not had to either lay off staff, or increase borrowing.

By now the company was as flexible as any. Semco had been redesigned to adapt to change, and to do so quickly without preconceived solutions or barriers. The particular approach at Ipiranga enabled the company to survive a national and sectoral recession, and to provide the basis on which full flexibility of work, and a fully flexible organization structure, could be developed.

KEY INSIGHTS

» The commitment of top management.
» The need for a "flexible working champion" – someone with the vision, direction, enthusiasm and energy to make the practices work.
» The contribution of flexible working to business excellence.
» The relationship between crisis and change management – in this case, using flexible working as the catalyst.
» The key management feature of never asking anybody to do anything that they themselves were not prepared to do.
» The generation of flexible attitudes and the returns available.
» Attention to the hard elements – the need for profitability and commercial effectiveness; the need for attention to costs.
» The position of flexible working in the process of organization development and enhancement.

Key Concepts and Thinkers

» Glossary of terms.
» Related concepts and thinkers.

A GLOSSARY FOR FLEXIBLE WORKING

Climate – The general feelings and perceptions felt by staff and others when within an organization.

Culture – The amalgam and summary of collective and individual attitudes, values and beliefs, and their relationship with ways of working.

Deregulation – Governmental, legal and statutory approaches to removing constraints and restrictions upon the employment of staff.

Employability – The development of skills, knowledge, attitudes, values and expertise in the pursuit of flexibility and capability within an organization; and to improve prospects in professional and occupational labor markets.

EU – The European Union; the EU issues directives, statutes and statutory instruments to which all employers operating within member states are required to comply; and advice, which is to encourage employers to adopt the highest possible standards of social and ethical practice.

Flexible working – Corporate and collective attitudes to deploying skills, knowledge, attitudes and expertise in the best interests of all concerned.

Flexible hours – The practice of requiring people to work as and when necessary.

Job sharing – A UK-based initiative by which a full-time job is divided up between two (or very occasionally three) individuals so that the whole is effectively carried out.

Job rotation – The practice of moving people around from one job to another on a regular basis in order to keep them fresh and interested.

Job enlargement – The practice of developing, or allowing jobholders to develop, the capabilities and contribution present in a particular job.

Job enrichment – The practice of improving the quality of particular jobs in terms of professional, occupational and organizational development.

Job-and-finish – Piecework in which a particular volume of work is carried out and then the employee may leave.

Kaizen – A Japanese expression meaning "continuous development"; *kaizen* has become incorporated into the language of management through its adoption as a philosophy by Japanese manufacturing companies; the practice requires continuous attention to practices and procedures in order to ensure that they are constantly being developed and improved.

Night working – Designing work patterns around the requirement to work at night; this may either be on a regular or *ad hoc* basis; two views are taken either that night work should be as regular as possible to minimize the disruption to physical and social health and well-being; or that it should be shared out among all members of particular organizations and work groups so that everybody does their fair share.

Non-standard hours – An expression summarizing work patterns that do not take place on Mondays to Fridays between 9.00 am and 5.00 pm.

Organization development (OD) – Strategic approaches to corporate, collective and individual training and development.

Portable careers – The development of individual, professional, occupational and technological capability in order to become an attractive "commodity" to the labor market; and the necessity for individuals to develop these because lifetime guarantees of work are no longer available.

Regulation – Government-led legal and statutory obligations to provide minimum standards of pay, hours of work, conditions and levels of treatment while at work.

Rewards – Intrinsic rewards are those that accrue as the result of satisfaction, success, enhancement and development. Extrinsic rewards are financial and material.

Shifts – The division of hours of work into prescribed patterns.

Standard hours – Either Monday to Friday, 9.00 am to 5.00 pm; or other established working hours.

Twilight hours working – The practice of engaging people between 5.00 pm and 11.00 pm in the evening.

Working Hours Directive – The EU statutory instrument that prescribes the maximum number of hours that those working in the member states of the EU may be requested to work without a break.

Zero hours – Job definition without reference to the number of hours required, so that either full flexibility is achieved in that staff work on demand; or that work "takes as long as it takes" this is a particular issue for those in administrative, junior and middle management functions in bureaucracies and hierarchies.

RELATED CONCEPTS AND THINKERS

Work design

Most organizations are not designed, they grow; but not all organizations adapt equally well to the environment within which they grow. For survival, continual growth and development in organizations, as with individuals, it helps to know what you would like to be before you try to become it. Analysis of the ideal of what should be, when compared with the reality of what is, may be disillusioning but it is the proper starting point for improvement and planned change.

Organization structure includes the allocation of formal responsibilities and the rank, status and hierarchy of a typical organization chart. It also covers the linking mechanisms between roles, coordinating structures and management style.

Organizations tend towards uniformity for the following reasons.

» *The cheapness of standardization* – it costs less to produce and process standard forms and formats; and training and development for standard procedures is easier and cheaper too.
» *The need for interchangeability* – especially with operations which require the use of common procedures, so that interactions can be carried out according to standard protocols.
» *The need for process control* – in which systems are produced so that fluctuations in the requirements of departments, divisions, functions and activities can be reflected in the operations of others.
» *The need for standard products and services* – because many organizations need uniformity of output from a variety of sources. These have to be designed in terms and forms simple enough to ensure that everyone gets the same quality, volume and durability.
» *The need for specialization.*

» *The desire for central control* – driven by the requirement of senior managers to "know what is going on," and is a push towards uniformity or control, rather than results.

Diversity

Uniformity is under constant pressure from the need for diversity. Pressures for diversity include the following:

» *regional and market diversity*, in which organizations are required to serve different customers, in different ways according to locality (and they are also required to employ staff from different localities who bring different expectations with them); and

» *technological diversity* – and the ability with which different technologies within organizations can be harmonized and integrated.

Effective work design requires addressing each of these elements, and reconciling their different priorities and influence. If this is not achieved, stress is caused. Effective approaches to organization and work design are based on flexibility and positive and dynamic attitudes; and on a willingness of people to develop work structures rather than to be constrained within them.

Highlights

Books:

» Handy, C.B. (1970, 1990, 1996) *Understanding Organizations*. Penguin.

Customer relations

A key driver of all flexible working and positive and dynamic attitudes is the requirement to continually satisfy the organization's customers and clients. It is therefore essential to understand the different types of customer that may be present in any situation. These include the following.

» *Apostles.* Apostles demonstrate extreme loyalty. Apostles are delighted with particular services and products, and may come to identify with them. Apostles, in effect, carry out marketing functions for the organization. They are highly loyal and they tell their friends and relations.

» *Loyalists*. Loyalists form the most important component of the customer base. They require much less effort on their behalf than do apostles, and generate large volumes of repeat business. Loyalists are the true firm foundation for any customer base. Customers only become loyalists as the result of high-quality products and services delivered over a period of time. While it should be recognized that many loyalists become so on the basis of convenience, as well as satisfaction, their loyalty has to be maintained and enhanced to ensure that they do not, in time, find it more convenient to go elsewhere.

» *Mercenary*. Mercenaries are the hardest customers to deal with. They go for the cheapest or most convenient option. They are difficult to deal with because they may well be satisfied but are not loyal. The management of mercenary customers requires attention to what genuinely brought them to the organization in the first place, and what may subsequently make them leave; if this is pure price advantage or increased convenience on the part of a competitor, it may be very difficult to manage in isolation.

» *Hostages*. Hostages appear to be very loyal but that is only because they have no choice. Customers *have* to deal with a gas, electricity, water or transport provider, their choice is therefore limited. Organizations never know whether their customers are loyal or hostages until competitors and substitutes appear on the scene. They may demonstrate a form of pseudo-loyalty in which they profess themselves satisfied, only to move on instantly as soon as an alternative becomes available.

» *Defectors*. Defectors are those who used to be customers. Once a customer has defected and given their custom to another organization, it may well be difficult to recover the situation. Organizations consequently need to ensure that complaints are dealt with as quickly and effectively as possible so that temporary dissatisfaction does not lead to defection.

» *Terrorists*. Terrorists, in customer relations terms, are the worst nightmare. In many cases, terrorists were apostles or loyalists until they were let down and the situation was not recovered. They are not so much dissatisfied with the organization's product or service as at war with it. They have a desire for revenge and retribution. On being let down, they have no problem in letting the world know about it; and many of those who appear on consumer affairs television programs have been previous apostles and loyalists.

A key feature of flexible working is therefore to understand the customers and clients as fully as possible, and to recognize the point of view from which they come to the organization. This is a key contribution to effective product and service delivery, and a major advance in the development of the knowledge, expertise and understanding required in order to remain effective.

Highlights

Books:

» Cartwright, R. (2000) *Mastering Customer Relations*. Palgrave.
» Jones, T. and Strasser, W. (1995) "Why satisfied customers defect," *Harvard Business Review*, Nov/Dec, pp. 88–99.

Intrapreneuring

Intrapreneur is the name given to enterprising individuals in successful businesses. Identifiable within this concept are two main strands: the characteristics of individuals who can be developed as intrapreneurs, and the nature of organizations that can develop them.

The characteristics identified as being essential within individuals are:

» commercial insight, and market and environmental awareness and understanding;
» personal strength of character and persistence in the approach to business matters and issues;
» professional and occupational stamina and staying power;
» innovative and creative approaches to problems, and the development of individual and collective creative faculties;
» the ability to accept, manage and direct change;
» the capacity for analysis, organization and direction of activities; and

» the ability to get on with people at all levels, to animate them and encourage others to perform their jobs effectively and successfully.

Organizations must have the following attributes:

» the ability to recognize the talent and potential of individuals and to harness these in mutually beneficial and profitable activities;
» the ability to learn and develop more quickly than the rate of organizational change, and to use the individual and collective energy thus generated as a force for change; and
» the capacity to provide both intrinsic and extrinsic rewards and opportunities commensurate with profit and individual capability.

The overall purpose is the creation of an environment where both business activities and talented individuals can come together for the generation of successful, dynamic and profitable ventures. Effective intrapreneuring is dependent on fully flexible attitudes and behavior; and the integration of development activities to provide corporate, positive, flexible and dynamic responses to opportunities and problems.

Highlights
Books:

» Lessem, R.S. (1990) *Global Management Principles*. Prentice Hall International.
» Pinchot, G. (1984, 1999) *Intranpreneuring*. John Wiley.

Alienation
Alienation is the term used to describe feelings such as the following.

» *Powerlessness* – arising from the inability to influence work conditions, volume, quality, speed and direction.
» *Meaninglessness* – arising from the inability to recognize the individual contribution made to the total.
» *Isolation* – which may be either physical or psychological. Physical alienation factors arise from work organization that requires people to be located in ways that do not allow for human interaction and feelings of mutual identity and interest. Psychological factors refer

to the relationship between different professions, occupations and activities; and staff groups and locations. Psychological distance is also affected by rank, status and hierarchy.

A combination of physical and psychological distance is generated among those who work away from the organization for long periods of time.

» *Low feelings of self-esteem and self-value* – arising from the lack of respect placed on staff by the organization, and its managers. Knowledge, belief and perceptions that those on standards patterns of work are both held in greater esteem, and also more highly rewarded than those on flexible and non-standard patterns.

» *Lack of prospect or advancement for the future* – feelings of being stuck or trapped in a situation purely for economic gain (and this is reinforced where wage levels are low).

» *General rejection* – based on adversarial, managerial and supervisory style.

» *Lack of meaningful communications, participation and involvement.*

» *Knowledge, belief and perception of lack of equality* – especially where the organization is seen to differentiate between different types and grades of staff to the benefit of some, and detriment of others.

Alienation is the major fundamental cause of conflicts and disputes at places of work. It is potentially present in all work situations. Those who wish to engage in effective flexible working arrangements must address each of these points as a key contribution to ensuring that the conditions, working environment, and management style are suitable and meet the needs of those on non-standard patterns of work and attendance.

Highlights

Books:

» Pettinger, R. (1996) *Introduction to Organizational Behaviour*. Macmillan.
» Luthans, F. (1994) *Organizational Behaviour*. McGraw-Hill.
» Ouchi, W.G. (1999) *Theory Z*. Avon.

Resources for Flexible Working

The chapter looks at the contributions of:

» Lessem
» Shefsky
» Hamel
» R. and A. Nissen
» Sternberg
» McConnell.

Each of the following represents a key contribution to both research and implementation of flexible working practices, and the advantages to both organizations and also individuals that successful activities bring.

The core element running throughout is investment – of energy, commitment, ambition and enthusiasm, as well as time and finance – in which returns are clearly anticipated and required. This reinforces the points made in Chapter 3 that flexible working is neither a means to cut corners nor to reduce total investment as a matter of expediency. Flexible working is a key contribution to maximizing and optimizing long-term returns on investment in each of these elements, and thereby contributing to enhanced organization performance.

Each of these resources approaches flexible working from a different point of view. These are:

» personal commitment;
» entrepreneurial commitment;
» academic scrutiny;
» virtual opportunities;
» moral and ethical drives; and
» the activist approach.

At the end of the chapter there is a list of further reading.

R.S. LESSEM

» *Intrapreneurship* (Wildwood House, 1990)

Personal commitment

The approach taken here is that flexible working is a direct necessity and consequence of engaging in productive and profitable commercial activities. The approach is complex, requiring a range of skills, knowledge, expertise and characteristics as follows.

» There is a need for *innovation*, so that organizations, work practices and industrial and commercial norms may be transformed.
» There is also a need for *design*, so that products and services can be given a real and perceived range of enhancements and improvements.

» There must be *leadership*, in which profitability and productivity are the function of those with strategic and policy capabilities.

» There must be *entrepreneurship*, in all organizations however long established, so that new products and services, and enhancements to existing products and services, can be both developed for the satisfaction of existing customers, and also introduced to new markets, sectors and locations.

» There must be a *change agency*. This is reflected in the need for constant improvement in existing practices, and in the drive to maximize and optimize the talents of those who are not able to attend regular and standardized patterns of work in conventional organizations; or to develop new and effective ways of working so that organizational and individual priorities are satisfied.

» There must be *animation*, in which life is brought to organizations. Lessem refers to animation as applying both to business organizations in their routines and activities, and to the attention required for the development of organizational climate, culture, myth and ritual. Each requires the establishment from the top of organizations rather than being allowed to emerge piecemeal.

» There must be *adventuring*, or the need for organizations and those who work within them to take leaps of faith from time to time. It also means a receptiveness to ideas from wherever in the world these may be discovered.

Lessem uses examples to illustrate each of the approaches – both individuals who have started up and made successful their own organizations (e.g. Anita Roddick with Body Shop, and Nelli Eichner of Interlingua), and those who work within organizations (e.g. John Harvey-Jones at ICI).

Attention is drawn to the qualities and capabilities required. Almost without exception, these require capability, flexibility and willingness of the overall approach; and qualities of flexibility, dynamism and responsiveness in all those who seek industrial, commercial – and public service – success.

Attention is drawn to the need for:

» hard work, the sheer physical and mental effort required to make things happen;

» managing the context in which hard work takes place, requiring especial attention to healthcare, stress management, and physical well-being;
» the need for discipline and the key corporate tasks of decision-making, planning, strategy development, process renewal and the establishment of aims and objectives as marks of achievement and direction; and
» creating shared values and identifiable positive and strong corporate cultures, with attention to social roles and meanings, as well as workplace demands.

Lessem states:

"As change agent and leader, a professionally managed organization can be established. One element is required to design and implement specialized systems and methods, the other is charged with devising and maintaining overall business strategy, organization structure, culture and purpose. Most people feel reasonably familiar with these elements. The flexible change agent and authoritative leader in fact take us to the limit of conventional wisdom within a managed organization."

The key to developing these further is the adoption of practices driven to secure high levels of staff motivation, commitment, identity and loyalty as a precursor to successful business development.

L.E. SHEFSKY

» *Entrepreneurs are Made not Born* (McGraw-Hill, 1998)

The entrepreneurial contribution to flexible working

"When you ask people what they do for a living, don't you react differently to the following response: 'I manage a chain of four stores,' than you do to a person who says: 'The business I started and own now consists of four stores?' Almost everyone finds entrepreneurs exciting for several reasons.

» Entrepreneurs are the prototype of the American persona. Unlike managers, entrepreneurs have an added dimension. Just having the determination to follow their dreams entitles them to respect and admiration.

» Businesses, meet your creator: there is something godlike about creativity, and entrepreneurs are creators. Managers create profits only from existing business. Entrepreneurs are not omnipotent but their ability to create a business where none existed is reason for respect, even awe.

» Entrepreneurial passion is catching. Entrepreneurs are passionate about their dreams and they transmit this to others. That is how they make things happen.

» Entrepreneurs cannot contain themselves. Entrepreneurs promote their businesses continually even when they are not actively selling. They are like proud parents showing off their baby's pictures. You may not care about their particular baby, but their passion about it, and the miracle of its birth, may infect you.

» Entrepreneurs are the Sinatra's of business. If you are an entrepreneur, you get to do it your way. Frank Sinatra's hit song, 'My Way', was not a big hit just because of Sinatra's great voice and delivery. He sold the song by embodying its spirit in his lifestyle. People enjoyed – perhaps even envied – Sinatra as he boldly proclaimed that he did things his way and loved it. People feel the same way about entrepreneurs. We respect and admire entrepreneurs for marching to their own tune which is not '9 to 5.'''

From the particular point of view of studying business start-ups, Shefsky's contribution to flexible working is based on the need for combining energy and enthusiasm with hard commercial realities and opportunities. The lessons apply to all those who wish to develop successful organizations, whether entrepreneurs or managers.

Attention is drawn to particular barriers that have to be overcome, and to the fact that these may be perceived to be insurmountable under different sets of circumstances. These must be attacked from the point of view that, if they cannot be surmounted, a route around them will be found. Particular attention is drawn to the following.

» *Fear of failure.* This is identified as a human condition, and one which carries greater stigma in different cultures; the worst failure is identified as being that which accrues from not tackling the issue at all.

» *Risk.* The need to generate a collective, as well as individual understanding of what risk actually entails, and the consequent requirement to use all parts of an organization to generate as much information as possible so that "risk based on ignorance or fear" is minimized or removed altogether.

At the core of the entrepreneurial approach is the "entrepreneur's work ethic." The need is to ensure that everyone involved is both capable and willing to undertake whatever duties are required, and to do this whenever, and wherever, it becomes necessary. Above all, the development of the required levels of flexibility and dynamism must be based on unqualified corporate support, and be led by those at the top of the organization.

G. HAMEL

» *Leading the Revolution* (Harvard Business School Press, 2000)

The academic perspective

Hamel's academic approach takes the form of strategic analysis and evaluation. He identifies principles of radical innovation and where new business ideas and concepts come from. Then he details the steps that companies must take towards innovation and enduring capability. The companies studied include Cisco, Virgin, Sears Roebuck, Walmart, Compaq, and Dupont, and examples are drawn from many other sources.

At the core of the argument lie five questions.

"Have we let others define customer expectations?"

"Did competitors see us more as rule takers or rule breakers?"

"Has our strategy changed in some important way in the last two years?"

"Has there been any erosion of our price premium or cost advantage?"

"Has it been more difficult to attract world class talent?"

The answer to the first four questions can be achieved only in full provided the fifth can be answered in the negative. The answers to these questions are then applied to re-establishing the following.

» The business mission which captures the overall objective of the strategy – what the business model is designed to accomplish or deliver.
» Product/market scope, capturing the essence of where the firm competes – for which customers, in which locations, and in what product and service segment; and where, by implication, it does not compete. Hamel states:

> "A company's definition of product/market scope can be a source of business concept innovation when it is quite different from that of traditional competitors."

» The basis for differentiation, capturing the essence of how the firm competes and, in particular, how it competes differently than its competitors. This can be followed up by assessing how competitors have tried to differentiate themselves in particular sectors, and other dimensions of differentiation that could be pursued.
» Strategic resources, which are identified as core competencies, strategic assets and core processes. The key to successful development of strategic resources lies in individual and collective core competencies. It is therefore essential that these be developed as far as possible so that what is achieved is unique, valuable to customers, and transferable to new opportunities. These can then be related to the exploitation of financial and technological assets and other resources, and in the development of the processes and procedures that support primary activities.

"Innovation solutions" can then be designed and implemented. These are dependent upon:

» the skills of those involved, especially in innovation;
» the potential of information technology to drive and enhance innovation – and again, reinforced by the capabilities of those using it;

» management processes required for effective innovation – and this is dependent upon the expertise with which management has been, and is being currently, developed.

R. NISSEN AND A. NISSEN

» *The Real Virtual Office* (Business Publications, 2000)

The virtual contribution

For expanding business, virtual working can enable low-cost and controlled expansion. An IT hardware company was developing fast. Its seven employees were stretched. The phone rang and rang and, as is so often the case, whoever was walking past at the time took the call. The result was increasing chaos. Prospective customers found the company's phone to be regularly and annoyingly engaged. Meetings and appointments were planned in haphazard fashion. The company contemplated a new switchboard and employing a full-time receptionist. This would have been the conventional thing to do. Instead it went virtual. Instead of paying $25,000 or more a year for a receptionist, the company outsourced its telephone reception answering service at a cost of $400 per month. Calls are diverted to receptionists armed with a database of diary entries and the latest whereabouts of key employees.

The answers to these problems were supplied by The Virtual Office, a company led by British entrepreneurs, Richard and Anthony Nissen. The name may be familiar – their father invented the Nissen Hut during World War I, the first mass produced prefabricated building. Later Richard Nissen was involved in his father's business, making and selling Lurex. An inventive and entrepreneurial strain clearly runs through the family.

This is an example of the networking and federating approach adopted by many organizations in different locations and sectors. Rather than including all functions under the same roof, the approach is to outsource as many activities as possible. Each activity is covered by a service level contract arrangement or agreement in return for which a price is paid. The potential for this approach is limited only by the attitudes adopted by the top managers of organizations. In many parts of the world, this has led to the contracting out of safety, catering and occupational health; now others are looking to do this for as many non-core functions as possible. The result is that for many organizations going through rapid growth of business development, or rapid expansion into new markets and sectors, all non-core functions can be farmed out and an agreed price/service level achieved (see Summary box 9.1).

SUMMARY BOX 9.1: PRICE PRITCHETT INC.

Price Pritchett Inc. is a change management and work restructuring consultancy. Based in Dallas, Texas, it produces a range of short, easy to read and accessible staff, management, and organizational handbooks on a wide range of positions that affect flexible working.

The organization deals extensively with work implications in virtual, networked and federated organizations and arrangements; with the employment considerations of mergers and acquisitions; and with identifying and managing the potential for stress that is caused in each of these situations.

Further information is available from www.pricepritchett.com.

E. STERNBERG

» *Just Business: Business Ethics in Action* (Warner, 1996)

Moral and ethical aspects

Sternberg identifies a range of corporate responsibilities and obligations for all aspects of the conduct of business. Of particular concern are the responsibilities and obligations to staff. An ethical approach is based on the following.

» Acknowledging the range of pressures and priorities that exist in the life of everyone, including health, family, social, ethical and religious pressures, as well as those related to work. The outcome of this is a full understanding of why employees think and behave in the ways that they do. Of particular concern is the potential for stress in all work situations; and this is compounded where there is uncertainty of continuity of work or economic rewards and returns.

» Confidentiality and integrity in all dealings with staff. This is the cornerstone on which all effective staff relationships are built. Where confidences are not kept, or where sensitive personal and occupational information become public property, the relationship is tainted and often destroyed. Confidentiality encourages people to be frank, open and honest themselves, and this leads to a genuine understanding of issues much more quickly. In flexible and non-standard patterns of work, the relationship is further damaged or diluted by the absence of familiar and frequent patterns of supervision and contact.

» Respect for individuals based on the value of their contribution to the organization. If they bring no value, they should not be there in the first place. Again, the pressure here is compounded for those on non-standard patterns of work – and requires especial attention to current job, future prospects, continuity of working relations, creation of suitable working environment, and maintenance of effective occupational and personal relationships, whatever the pattern of attendance or hours of work.

Sternberg bases her approach on the following.

» *distributive justice*, a fundamental equality of approach, opportunity and treatment regardless of length of service or hours worked; and
» *ordinary common decency*, in which people behave towards each other in "the correct" and "right" ways in all dealings.

The cost of disregarding ordinary common decency and distributive justice is characterized by lying, cheating and stealing. Low morale typically replaces initiative and enthusiasm. Teamwork becomes difficult at best, and long-term commitments counterproductive.

C. MCCONNELL

» *Change Activist: Make Big Things Happen Fast* (Pearson Education, 2001)

The activist approach

McConnell identifies a principle called "change activism." Change activism is about taking control at a personal level: how to apply activist principles to working life so that people and organizations become more effective and successful. At the core of this is the need for individual proactive responsibility for, and development of, the skills and attitudes required. These are identified as:

» personal understanding of priorities;
» personal understanding of success and failure;
» personal passion and commitment; concentrating on things that are important and worthwhile;
» energy and persistence; and
» continuous education, training and skills and knowledge development.

Change activism has business benefits. Each of the elements above also requires applying in corporate situations. The key is to connect passionate, capable individuals with passionate, capable organizations; the consequence is that the constraints of "old ways" of doing things are lost and organizations and their staff are energized and empowered in the ways required.

The broader responsibility of change activism involves the drive towards ecological responsibilities, fundamental principles of equality for the population of the world, and the global increases in standards of civilization.

Overall, the approach "turns up the volume" on priorities and things that everyone cares about.

"Imagine your workplace filled with trust, getting a daily buzz doing something you really care about. Activists have a passionate connection to what needs to be done, and a huge sense of fulfillment because that is what happens when your work involves true contribution from the heart.

"We need change activism because of where we are. Do you feel valued at work? Do you know your current market value? Would you say you live a life true to your values?"

Organizations suffer from the inability to manage change effectively; and this is compounded by the fact that they are unable to find, recruit and retain those with the necessary qualities of tenacity, enthusiasm and ambition, combined with the expertise necessary to drive forward big change. Employees seeking fulfilling work and balance in their lives treat their organization as a form of expediency rather than commitment. The fundamental principles, relationships, and attitudes within organizations and between staff are therefore flawed and certain to produce only limited results.

The activist approach develops a true understanding of the broad context for everyone involved. This must start at the top of the organization with an active, commercial *and moral* commitment to the economic, social and ecological responsibilities that corporations and individuals are going to be required to address over the coming period.

FURTHER READING

Ash, M.K. (1990) *On People Management*. Sage.

Cartwright, R. (1994) In *Charge: Managing Yourself*. Blackwell.

– (2000) *Mastering Customer Relations*. Macmillan Palgrave.

Drucker, P.F. (2000) *Management Challenges for the 21st Century*. HarperCollins.

Griseri, P. (1996) *Managing Values*. Macmillan.

Hamel, G. (1998) *Competing for the Future*. The Free Press.

Handy, C. (1990) *The Age of Unreason*. Penguin.

– (1986) *The Future of Work*. Penguin.

Heller, R. (1998) *In Search of European Excellence*. HarperCollins.

Morita, A. (1986) *Made in Japan: The Sony Story*. Fontana.

Luthans, F. (1994) *Organizational Behaviour*. McGraw-Hill.

Pascale, R. & Athos, A. (1990) *The Art of Japanese Management*. Sage.

Peters, T. & Austin, N. (1986) *A Passion for Excellence*. Harper & Row.

Peters, T. & Waterman, R. (1982) *In Search of Excellence*. Harper & Row.

Pettinger, R. (1996) *Managing the Flexible Workforce*. Cassell.

– (1998) *Measuring Business and Managerial Performance*. Financial Times/Pearson.

– (2000) *Mastering Organizational Behaviour*. Macmillan Palgrave.

- (2001) *Mastering Management Skills*. Macmillan Palgrave.
Porter, M. (1980) *Competitive Strategy*. The Free Press.
- (1986) *Competitive Advantage*. The Free Press.
Roddick, A. (1994) *Body and Soul: The Body Shop Story*. Ebury.
Semler, R. (1992) *Maverick*. Century Business.
- (1998) *The Maverick Solution*. BBC.
Senge, P. (1992) *The Fifth Discipline*. Century Business.
Wickens, P. (1996) *The Road to Nissan*. Macmillan.
- (2000) *The Ascendant Organization*. Macmillan.

Ten Steps to Effective Flexible Working

The 10 steps to a successful learning organization are in summary:

1 Responsiveness to change
2 Effective communications
3 Management style
4 Work structures
5 Recognizing achievements
6 Responsibility and accountability
7 Expectations
8 Ethical position
9 Motivation and morale
10 Continuous improvement and development.

Flexibility and flexible working come from an attitude, a culture, a corporate state of mind; and from engaging the capabilities, attitudes and qualities of the staff, and then combining them into productive and acceptable patterns of work. The outcome is organizational forms and staffing approaches filled by people who are prepared, willing and able to do more than those placed in straightjacketed, formalized job descriptions and work patterns outside which they never stray. The following issues therefore require attention.

1. RESPONSIVENESS TO CHANGE

The major return on investment on strategic approaches to flexible working is the ability to respond to change. Provided that the high-quality/high-value/high-pay equation is committed to, and delivered, organizations and their senior managers are fully entitled to expect positive, flexible and responsive attitudes from their staff, whatever their present occupation, length of service, patterns and hours of work.

So long as this is reinforced with full consultation, both the capability and willingness to understand why things have to change is fully instilled in everyone. Primarily, this means having the capacity to address the behavioral barriers to change as follows.

» *Fear of the unknown.* Changes which confront people with the unknown tend to cause stress, anxiety and fear. The status quo suddenly becomes "the perfect" way of work and life organization to the staff.
» *Security in the past.* People who have got into working habits tend to find comfort and security in these. Anything that disrupts the real and perceived order and stability is therefore to be resisted.
» *"There is no alternative" and "it must be done."* These are phrases used by senior corporate managers to drive changes through. Because they are then not adequately explained, resistance and uncertainty are created.
» *The position of vested interests and lobby groups.* When faced with change, especially that which is likely to lead to their loss of influence, such groups spend time and energy producing rational,

pseudo-rational and spurious arguments as to why change should not take place.

» *Career paths.* Those on career paths, and whom the present status quo serves extremely well, tend to resist when this is disrupted.

In each of these cases, a full flexibility of attitude and culture, as well as working practices, are likely to address many of the concerns raised. Physical barriers such as technological change, relocation and redeployment also ought to be less of a problem, because:

» the corporate attitude ensures that people address these issues positively; and
» full support is given to retraining and technical, professional and occupational development as required.

The opportunities in the status quo are therefore replaced with alternatives, rather than being removed altogether.

2. EFFECTIVE COMMUNICATIONS

All flexible work patterns need support and the key to this is effective communications. This means:

» understanding the needs of those on non-standard patterns of work and working away from the organization's locations;
» providing the means by which information is best presented, transmitted, received and understood;
» engaging managers and supervisors in facetoface meetings with staff whenever possible or required; and
» prioritizing managerial and supervisory workloads to ensure that the people have sufficient time and resources to maintain regular contact with their staff.

This must include "managing by ringing and e-mailing around"; and must in-build visits to those at alternative locations, or on twilight night and weekend working. Managers and supervisors must be available when members of staff do come into the office and need to see them.

In general, the best way of managing communications is to ensure that staff are told what they must, should and ought to know, either face to face or over the telephone; and this is then followed up with paper or e-mail summaries. Effective flexible work management requires this as a major priority (see Summary box 10.1).

SUMMARY BOX 10.1: MISPERCEPTIONS

The two major misperceptions of those who supervise flexible staff are the following.

» "The staff want to be left alone to get on with their job"

This is often true, especially for field sales staff, consultants and other experts. However, they still need to do it in context, and so that they continue to understand organizational activities and priorities, as well as the demands of their own workloads.

» "They are only here for a few hours and we cannot waste time doing this"

Again, the first part of this may be true. Problems arise when the second part becomes a corporate attitude. This leads to under-valuing the non-standard workforce relative to everyone else, and at the very least, a perceived variation in standards of treatment and respect.

3. MANAGEMENT STYLE

Many organizations that adopt flexible working practices require a fundamental shift in management style alongside the implementation of new workplace approaches. Flexible working is effective in all situations – autocratic, participative, democratic, bureaucratic – provided that there is visibility, frequency and constancy of contact. This means maintaining the standards and forms of regular contact as indicated above. It also means ensuring that top managers, as well as supervisors and section heads, regularly get round to see all of their staff, and the activities that take place at non-standard times (e.g. nights, weekends and twilight) (see Summary box 10.2).

SUMMARY BOX 10.2: THE MANAGEMENT OF NON-STANDARD WORK PATTERNS

The good: Walmart Inc.

S.M. Walton, the founder of Walmart, the largest supermarket chain in the world, used to make sure that he visited all of his staff at least once a year. He used to meet those working on night shifts restocking the shelves and loading and unloading trucks during their periods of work. He would arrive with trays of doughnuts and coffee for all those present. Everyone would then have the opportunity to meet the person for whom they worked; and he would listen to their concerns and address them.

The bad: The UK National Health Service (NHS)

The Walmart approach may be contrasted with the almost complete lack of contact between medical, nursing and emergency services in the UK, and those for whom they ultimately work. It is an enduring problem with service maintenance and staff morale, as well as the delivery of professional expertise, that no senior managers, health department bureaucrats or functional supervisors ever actually see for themselves how work is carried out, or the prevailing conditions at non-standard times. This has led to great problems of psychological distance between those responsible for medical and nursing practice, and those whose job it is to manage and direct the service.

Sources: Peters, T. & Austin, N. (1986) *A Passion for Excellence*. Harper & Row; and Statt, D. (1998) *Organizational Psychology*. Macmillan.

4. WORK STRUCTURES

The overriding principle is to ensure that there is a sufficient volume and value of work in patterns that combine regularity, frequency and commitment. The ideal is to ensure that attendance, output and identity all contribute to:

» mutual understanding, respect and value;
» effective and understood work achievement; and
» productive and positive working habits.

Those who work as follows therefore require particular attention.

» Seasonal staff require induction into any changes that have taken place since they were last present. This includes meeting new colleagues, managers and supervisors, as well as job training in changed equipment or technology.

» Temporary staff, whether expert or general, need to understand how, where, why and for how long their expertise or capability is to be applied, and the constraints that may affect this.

» Those working away from headquarters need extended induction periods to build behavioral identity and confidence, as well as knowledge of procedures and practices, before they are turned loose on their customer and client bases, and colleagues elsewhere.

» Working hours structures need to combine attention to effective performance with a recognition of the human issues present. For example, cleaners attending organizations for one hour per day can be provided with proper contact provided that there is corporate willingness to do so; those attending for one hour per week are much less likely to have any identity and it is not clear what contribution this minute level of attendance would have.

» Those on "attendance when required" patterns are giving of their own personal flexibility and this needs to be reciprocated in terms of commitment and intrinsic and extrinsic rewards.

» Those required to work regular, non-standard patterns (e.g. nights, weekends) should be given enough operational structure to build up patterns of attendance, effectiveness of work output, and physical adjustment. Night shifts, especially, should never be *ad hoc* or split with non-night demands during periods of work. To do so is physically damaging to health; and there are also knock-on effects on psychological and social confidence.

5. RECOGNIZING ACHIEVEMENTS

Everyone should be given recognition regardless of patterns of attendance or hours of work. This sounds trite; it is nevertheless true that those who attend regular and standard hours gain greater recognition and better opportunities that those who do not. This reinforces the need for a visible and proactive management and supervisory style, designed around all patterns of work. Problems arise with motivation and morale when those on non-standard patterns come to believe either that they are working in isolation, or that their achievements are being taken for granted or suffocated by those produced elsewhere.

This therefore reinforces the need for effective, collective and corporate communications, as well as attention to individual requirements. Everyone likes to know that their successes have been widely recognized; that their problems will be addressed positively; and this is reinforced when it is known, believed or perceived that recognition is available elsewhere in the organization.

Recognizing the achievements of everyone helps to break down barriers that may exist (or at least have the potential to exist) between professions and occupations, and between those on different patterns and locations of work.

6. RESPONSIBILITY AND ACCOUNTABILITY

Effective non-standard attendance hours and locations of work require ensuring that all those involved understand the extent of their authority, responsibility and accountability. They need to know when, where and to whom to go for support and advice, and to solve problems.

Such problems are increased if nobody in authority can be contacted during non-standard working hours. They are reduced if either they can be contacted, or if authority is devolved so that those actually present can take matters into their own hands, and address issues as they see fit, in the certain knowledge that they will receive full support.

The first duty is to ensure that rewards are paid for acceptance of responsibility and accountability. The second is to ensure that corporate, collective, individual, professional, occupational and personal commitments are clearly understood. If individuals are overtly acting in the name of the organization, they need to know that they are doing this right and that their actions will be supported at all times. This reinforces the need for:

» a fully supportive style of management in which those in authority effectively act as a resource and service for those at the frontline; and

» continuous staff training and development in practical problem-solving in all activities, in product and service quality, in customer management, and in staff management and labor relations activities.

The emphasis must be on quick and effective actions with which those directly affected are satisfied, and which can be accommodated within the organization.

The approach is designed to ensure that the greatest possible autonomy, flexibility and responsibility in dealings with the customers and clients is achieved. The primary responsibility of managers and supervisors is therefore to support and develop frontline capability. If this is effectively structured and institutionalized, responsibility, authority and accountability are both understood and also assured.

7. EXPECTATIONS

Effective flexible working demands that the expectations of everyone concerned are understood and addressed. It is therefore necessary to understand the following.

» Customers and clients come to the organization for products and services at times suitable to themselves; they therefore expect a uniformly high-quality service, whatever the time of day or night.
» Staff expect to be able to enjoy a good quality of working life and environment, as well as producing valuable and worthwhile work.
» Staff expect to be able to deliver their commitment to their organization while balancing other demands on their lives.
» Staff expect increasing levels of intrinsic and extrinsic rewards in return for their output, capability and commitment.
» Staff expect a fundamental decency and equality of treatment and opportunity.

The clear emphasis is, therefore, that customer and client expectations can be managed effectively only so long as high levels of commitment are made to the staff if product and service quality are to be assured in the long term. The right conditions have to be created, and expertise developed, so that what is required by customers and clients is delivered regardless of the time or day of the week. There is clearly a direct relationship between attention to staff expectations, and standards and quality of work that can be expected. If the attention to staff expectations is correct, then organizations, and their managers, are entitled to expect high levels of volume and quality of work in return.

8. ETHICAL POSITION

This is a key feature of organization culture and climate. Attention is required to organization and operational policies, practices and procedures so that the ways in which people behave are:

» positive, not negative;
» right, not wrong or expedient;
» driven by high absolute standards of attitude and value; and
» considerate of local, social and religious customs and other pressures.

The overarching values of the organization are required to produce a culture that is:

» designed, not emergent – in which standards of attitude, behavior and performance are set and established and not allowed to emerge by default;
» strong, not weak – to which everyone is required to subscribe – and which often means that the organization will not be all things to all people;
» flexible and dynamic, rather than inert or becalmed – and this begins with the attitudes and values exhibited by top managers and the extent to which these are fully inclusive, or whether they concentrate on some groups of staff at the expense of others.

The ethical position is again underpinned by fundamental standards of equality of treatment and opportunity for all. Attention is also necessary to ensure that principles of management and supervision are designed, developed and implemented so that everyone is treated in the same way as they conduct their work.

9. MOTIVATION AND MORALE

Having established high absolute standards, the key to maintaining collective and individual motivation and morale is recognizing and attending to those elements that potentially damage or destroy productive and harmonious working conditions. This means paying primary attention to those factors that, if either wrong or not present, lead to extreme dissatisfaction at work. Herzberg, in his book *Work and the Nature of Man* (Granada, 1960), identified these as:

- » company policy and administration;
- » supervision and management style;
- » levels of pay and salary;
- » relationships with peers;
- » relationships with subordinates;
- » status; and
- » job, work and occupational security.

These are factors that, where they are good and adequate, do not in themselves make people satisfied; on the other hand, where these aspects are bad, extreme dissatisfaction is more or less universally experienced.

There are specific requirements in each area if effective flexible working is to be implemented. Administrative policies and practices must recognize the value and contribution of those on flexible conditions, rather than operating in isolation from them. As stated throughout, pay and reward levels must be sufficiently high to place a value and respect on the work carried out, as well as a substantial economic return. Relationships between those on flexible work patterns, especially those operating in isolated locations, must be developed and enhanced wherever possible, using whatever means are available (including electronic). Relationships between individuals and other work groups must also be developed so that mutual general understanding at least is achieved. Again, failure to do this leads to perceptions of isolation and alienation on the part of those on flexible and non-standard working patterns.

Positive initiatives in motivation can then be developed to ensure:

- » work satisfaction based on enrichment, opportunity and variety;
- » high levels of team, group and organizational identity;
- » positive, professional and occupational relationships between group members, as well as between different groups and teams;

» attitudes that learn from failure, rather than seeking to apportion blame; and

» relating status to work performance and output, rather than job titles, status, group or department membership.

If all of this is in place, organizations are entitled to accept a reciprocal commitment from their employees, high levels of motivation, and high standards and quality of work.

10. CONTINUOUS IMPROVEMENT AND DEVELOPMENT

At a strategic level, flexible working reflects the continuous drive for improvements in product and service output and quality. At an operational level, this is achieved through establishing and developing the required levels of performance from everyone, regardless of location, occupation or hours worked.

In practice, this reinforces the need for establishing the management and supervisory styles that the situation demands. It is not otherwise easy to enthuse those on irregular patterns of work to perform to high levels. This is reinforced if there are known, believed or perceived differentials in the esteem and value in which different categories of staff are held.

Performance measurements and appraisal training and development, and other activities, are therefore developed on the basis that they are universal and fully inclusive. Core training programs – induction, job training, health and safety, emergency procedures, technological proficiency, and attention to behavior and demeanor – are delivered to everyone as a primary element of developing the skills and attitudes required for effective long-term flexible working.

This enhances expectations all round. Again, it is not always easy to implement with those staff who are working as second income earners, or to fit in with other commitments. Physically, it is not always easy to get those working in isolated or autonomous situations to reschedule their work in order to fit in with such activities. To be fully effective, therefore, these initiatives require long-term scheduling and a high value placed and anticipated if they are to be fully effective.

Moreover, it is necessary to establish levels of attitude and performance at the outset and to build on these during the initial period of employment. Those who come with low expectations need to have these repositioned. In return, the relationship between expectations, efforts and rewards must be confirmed (see Fig. 6.1 in Chapter 6).

The organization's obligation is first to ensure that rewards are forthcoming; and subsequently, to develop all three elements for all concerned. This must apply regardless of rank, status, location, hours or patterns of work, or initial individual job expectations.

CONCLUSIONS

Flexible working requires a fundamental shift of traditional organizational approaches from the rigid and hierarchical to the pursuit of product and service quality and excellence. This is supported by high-quality human and labor relations, high levels of attention to product and service, and an understanding of what constitutes customer satisfaction.

Paradoxically, flexibility is conformist. It is based on high and distinctive prescribed standards of behavior, attitude, performance and commitment. Those who work in flexible organizations accept these – or do not work. If they are to be effective and successful, they must be capable of harmonizing staff and organization, of finding and developing mutuality of interest in the working situation.

Flexible working is an opportunity for:

» business to transform its activities and service quality;
» public services to get to grips with, often very limited, resources;
» managers to develop real management (as distinct from administrative and procedural) expertise;
» customers to extend their range of choice and opportunity; and
» staff – people from all walks of life – to realize their potential, pursue interests, lead varied, productive and rewarding working lives, and to harmonize these with everything else that is important to them.

Frequently Asked Questions (FAQs)

Q1: What exactly is "flexible working?"

A: Refer to Chapters 2 and 3.

Q2: How much will it save me?

A: Refer to Chapters 2, 6 and 10.

Q3: What are my liabilities? Can I be sued if I casualize all my staff?

A: Refer to Chapters 6 and 10.

Q4: Do I have to pay minimum wages for non-standard staff? Do they enjoy full protection and rights?

A: Refer to Chapters 3, 6, 7 and 10.

Q5: Can I lay staff off and insist that they work when it suits me?

A: Refer to Chapter 10.

Q6: How am I going to get the best out of staff who are only here on a casual basis?

A: Refer to Chapters 5-8.

Q7: How do I go about getting the most from my resources?

A: Refer to Chapters 5-7.

Q8: What activities can be put out to flexible working?

A: Refer to Chapters 5-10.

Q9: What attitudes should I adopt towards flexible workers?

A: Refer to Chapters 4, 5, 9 and 10.

Q10: How much will it cost me?

A: Refer to Chapters 2-5 and 10.

Index

Printed in the United States
By Bookmasters

Printed in the United States
By Bookmasters